POWER EVANGELISM

By the same authors:

POWER HEALING

POWER EVANGELISM

with Study Guide

John Wimber
and
Kevin Springer

HODDER

Scripture quotations are taken from THE HOLY BIBLE, NEW
INTERNATIONAL VERSION, copyright © 1973, 1978, 1984
by the International Bible Society. Used by permission.

Copyright © 1992 John Wimber and Kevin Springer

First published in Great Britain 1985
New edition with study guide first published 1992
This edition 2001

The right of John Wimber and Kevin Springer to be identified
as the author of the Work has been asserted by them in
accordance with the Copyright, Designs and Patents Act 1988.

10

British Library Cataloguing in Publication Data
A record for this book is available from the British Library

ISBN 978 0340 56127 0

Printed and bound in Great Britain by Clays Ltd, St Ives plc

The paper and board used in this paperback are natural
recyclable products made from wood grown in sustainable
forests. The manufacturing processes conform to the
environmental regulations of the country of origin.

Hodder & Stoughton
A Division of Hodder Headline Ltd
338 Euston Road
London NW1 3BH
www.madaboutbooks.com

CONTENTS

MY STORY

I knew little about God when I converted to Christianity in 1962. A fourth-generation unbeliever, I had received no Christian training as a child. As an adult I had neither belonged to nor regularly attended a church. At twenty-nine years of age, I was a jazz musician with a soaring career and a diving marriage. The reason for my conversion to Christianity was simple: my life was in a shambles and I was told a personal relationship with Jesus Christ offered hope from the despair. Certainly my conversion was not the result of sincere intellectual enquiry into the mysteries of God.

Carol, my wife, also committed her life to Christ in 1962. A young mother with three children and another on the way, she had to contend with my disorderly lifestyle and her own gnawing sense of guilt for having turned away from her Christian heritage. She had been raised in the Church and had attended Christian parochial schools. So, like me, she too turned to Christianity out of deep personal need, but, unlike mine, her conversion also had an intellectual component. Her questions – about God and Satan, heaven and hell, salvation and damnation – were many and urgent. For Carol, reasonable answers to these questions were the foundation of faith.

For both of us the results of our conversions were the same: freedom from guilt and the fear of death, a purpose for living, and a renewed marriage. We also immediately plunged into personal evangelism. There were so many who had not heard the gospel! Family members, friends, strangers – anyone willing to listen – heard the news of

Jesus from us. But soon it became apparent that Carol and I each approached evangelism differently, perhaps accounted for by our dissimilar backgrounds.

For Carol, a clear, logical presentation of the gospel was central to the evangelistic task. She wanted to answer all the questions (even when people were not asking them!), always aiming for a solid intellectual base to the conversion. I relied more on my intuition, a spiritual guidance system that told me when people were ready to give their lives to Christ. Frequently I interrupted Carol's presentations (much to her consternation) and asked the person we were talking with if he or she wanted to receive Jesus Christ at that very moment. Inevitably the person wanted to pray. Unlike Carol's, my basic assumption was that even with only minimal information about Christ, one may begin a personal relationship with him. Evangelism, I thought, did not necessitate passing on a great deal of information about Christ. But I was uneasy about how much knowledge was necessary for faith in Christ, and why some people needed so little while others needed more.

C. S. Lewis' conversion captures the interplay – and mystery – of faith and reason in the conversion process. Raised in the Anglican Church of Ireland, Lewis had no more than a nominal belief. By the time he was confirmed at age sixteen he considered himself an atheist, only attending church to please his father. As a schoolboy he was tutored by the renowned dialectician W. T. Kirkpatrick. Kirkpatrick was a professed atheist who trained Lewis to 'talk to victory' and always insisted on precision of terms and clarity of logic in his arguments.

After serving in the army during the First World War and completing his education at Oxford, Lewis was elected to a fellowship in English Language and Literature at Magdalen College, Oxford, a position he held for the next thirty years. It was at Oxford that Lewis came into contact with Christian intellectuals like Nevill Coghill, J. R. R. Tolkien and Owen Barfield. Later they, along with the novelist Charles Williams, would form the core of the 'Inklings', a group of Oxford dons who met weekly to read their writings aloud and discuss them. Through the quiet witness of the future Inklings and the influence of his own readings ('A young man who wishes to remain a sound atheist cannot be too careful of his reading,' he later wrote), Lewis slowly inched towards Christianity.

In 1929, at the age of thirty-two, he was converted to belief in a personal God. Later he wrote, 'Amiable agnostics will talk cheerfully about "man's search for God". To me, as I was then, they might as well have talked about a mouse's search for the cat.'

Even though he believed in God, for some time Lewis struggled with the claims of Jesus and the gospel. It was two years later, while he was riding to a local zoo in the sidecar of his brother Warren's motorcycle, that his conversion to Christ was completed. It was not a dramatic sort of conversion: all he could say later was, 'When we set out I did not believe that Jesus Christ is the Son of God, and when we reached the zoo I did.'

I have described C. S. Lewis' conversion to drive home a point: after all the years of doubting and seeking, debate and reading, for no apparent reason, in the sidecar of a motorcycle, he believed in Christ. His search had been important, but in the end it took no more than a motorcycle ride with his brother to complete his conversion. His time of faith had come.

As a pastor in the late 1960s and early 1970s, I continued to feel a tension between the intellectual and intuitive aspects of the evangelistic task. Then, in 1974, shortly after joining the staff of the Charles E. Fuller Institute of Evangelism and Church Growth in Pasadena, California, I learned about the 'Engel Scale', a model that describes the various stages in thinking (from little knowledge to a lot) and attitudes (from hostile to responsive) that people frequently go through in conversion. This was a hallmark for me, because James F. Engel's research demonstrated that in most societies there is always a group of people who are on the verge of converting to Christianity, and their openness to it involves both intellectual and attitudinal factors. Further, Dr Engel asserted that the most effective type of evangelism aims at this group. C. S. Lewis, when he went on his motorcycle trip to the zoo, was on the verge, ready for harvesting. As a young Christian I had a knack for identifying members of that open group and leading them to Christian commitment. The Engel Scale helped me understand who these people were and why aiming only at their intellects was not the most effective way to evangelise them.

So Carol and I were both right. For effective evangelism there must be the message, the content of the gospel: 'Faith comes from hearing the message, and the message is heard through the word of Christ' (Rom. 10:17). And there must also be right timing – the person must be ready, ripened for harvest. Among most Western evangelicals, the intellectual task is frequently stressed to the exclusion of the intuitive.

Also around this time I was introduced to C. Peter Wagner's writings on the goals of personal evangelism. Dr Wagner points out that too often Western evangelicals' goal is merely to help people make a *decision* to follow Christ, whereas the great commission passage in Matthew 28:19–20 calls for the making of full disciples: Christians who not only believe but are trained and living out the demands of the gospel. This confirmed my suspicion that many evangelicals place a priority on the intellectual aspects of the gospel that often results in a confusion of intellectual assent (knowing *about* Christ) with faith itself, and of right thinking with right living.

This is not to belittle the importance of the Christian mind and good theology. A central task of evangelism is the bold proclamation of the gospel, a clear and precise presentation of the death, burial and resurrection of Christ. But for this message to be heard and understood there must be more than the dissemination of information. Dr Wagner calls the making of disciples the result of persuasion evangelism. Well into the 1970s I was still confused about how consistently to practise persuasion evangelism, evangelism that produces not just decisions but disciples of Christ. There had to be another element, a missing part, that would catalyse personal evangelism.

Then I was introduced to another of Dr Wagner's books, *Look Out! The Pentecostals Are Coming*. I had always avoided Pentecostal and charismatic Christians, in part because it seemed that often controversy and division surrounded their ministries. Also, my judgement of their ministries was coloured by a presupposition that charismatic gifts like tongues, prophecy and healing were not for today. (As a dispensationalist, I believed the charismatic gifts had ceased at the end of the first century.) But in Dr Wagner I encountered a credible witness, an accomplished missionary and dean of Fuller Theological Seminary's School of World Mission, who wrote that healing and deliverance from evil spirits were happening in South America today. Further, he proved that these miraculous encounters resulted in large evangelistic harvests and church growth. His book forced me to reconsider my position on the charismatic gifts, though I was still sceptical of their validity today.

With this new openness, I read books by Donald Gee (an English Pentecostal who wrote *Concerning Spiritual Gifts*) and Morton Kelsey (*Healing and Christianity*) on the charismatic gifts. Their writings, combined with first-person testimonies of the miraculous from Third World students at Fuller Theological Seminary's School of World Mission, opened me to a new understanding of the part the Holy Spirit plays in evangelism. While I did not agree with all that Gee and Kelsey wrote (and still do not), I had to reconsider much that I had been taught about the charismatic gifts.

I also re-evaluated my experiences in personal evangelism. Slowly I began to realise that my ability to know people's concerns and when they were ready to convert to Christ – what previously I thought were merely psychological insights – were possibly spiritual gifts like a word of

knowledge or a word of wisdom. I wondered, had I for
years been experiencing these spiritual gifts in my evangelistic efforts?

As I searched the Gospels to learn more about the gifts, I
discovered another significant point: Jesus always combined the proclamation of the kingdom of God with its
demonstration (the casting out of demons, healing the sick,
raising the dead, and so on). The spiritual gifts took on new
meaning for me. Scripture indicated that they authenti-
cated the gospel, cutting through people's resistance and
drawing attention to the good news of Jesus Christ. No
wonder Jesus was so effective in evangelism.

By 1977 my thinking regarding personal evangelism was
significantly altered. Once I accepted the fact that all the
spiritual gifts are for today, I found a key for effective
evangelism: combining the proclamation with demonstration of the gospel. (In fact, it is accurate to say that my
search for more effective evangelism led in part to the
spiritual gifts.) Rather than detracting from the proclamation of the gospel, the gifts, I observed, when correctly
practised, open people to a clearer understanding and
practice of Christianity. There is unusual power and effectiveness in this form of evangelism, which is the reason that
I call it 'power evangelism'.

While my understanding and practice of evangelism, the
Holy Spirit, and church growth were undergoing a revolu-
tion, I still lacked a biblical theology that integrated the
three, a grid for understanding how they are supposed to
work together and fulfil God's purpose on earth. This last
element – a solid, evangelical theology – is the foundation
on which all practice must stand. I was already acquainted
with George Eldon Ladd's writings (he was a Fuller Theological Seminary professor), but it was not until I read his
book *Jesus and the Kingdom* that I realised how his work on
the kingdom of God formed a theological basis for power
evangelism. As I read Dr Ladd's works, and then read
afresh the gospel accounts, I became convinced that power
evangelism was for today.

I do not believe that it is enough for Christians to gather information, understand new facts – even think differently about the supernatural in Scripture – if it does not affect how we live. At the core of my being I am an activist. Regarding power evangelism, this meant that I needed to field-test my new-found theology, to go out into the world and see if what I thought Scripture taught in fact worked in Western society. So in 1978 I left the Charles E. Fuller Institute of Evangelism and Church Growth to become pastor of what is now called the Vineyard Christian Fellowship of Anaheim, California. It was in this environment, a small group of fifty people, that I first tested my theories of power evangelism. Today that small group has grown into a movement of forty thousand people in a hundred and forty congregations around the United States and Canada. Many of the experiences described on the following pages are drawn from these congregations.

Though I write about power evangelism, the most powerful evangelism will come only when Jesus' prayer for Christian unity is fulfilled: 'May they be brought to complete unity to let the world know that you sent me and have loved them even as you have loved me' (John 17:23). I pray that what I write about power evangelism will contribute to that unity.

INTRODUCTION TO THE REVISED EDITION

When we wrote *Power Evangelism* we never imagined that it would generate such remarkable influence and sales. Terms in the book like power encounter, divine appointment, signs and wonders, and power evangelism itself are now common currency among Christians from a variety of traditions. Sales of *Power Evangelism* worldwide currently approach 250,000, and they continue growing. The book has been published in at least a dozen languages.

Power Evangelism, however, has produced more than sales and popularity. Countless reviews and books have been written in defence of or attacking its ideas. Seminaries and Bible schools have sponsored theological symposiums to debate the pros and cons of power evangelism. Theologians and pastors have excoriated or championed what even we admit are radical – though in no way novel – concepts surrounding the evangelistic task.

Due to all this attention, last year we decided to take another look at the book. *Power Evangelism* was originally published in England in 1985. We actually wrote it in 1984, working from notes developed in a course I (John Wimber) co-taught with C. Peter Wagner in the early 1980s at Fuller Theological Seminary in Pasadena, California. We thought that a second edition would be helpful to the reader for many reasons.

First, because *Power Evangelism* was our first book, we felt there were sections that should be re-written for greater clarity and easier reading. This was particularly true of the worldview chapter. We were also not satisfied with the book's format, so we re-organised it into sections and smaller chapters.

This latter change made the book more compatible with a Study Guide, which we have included in this new edition. The goal for all of our writings is to motivate and equip the reader to do the work of the kingdom – whether it be prayer, Bible study, praying for the sick, feeding the poor, or evangelising the lost. The Study Guide will help you to get out on the streets and share the good news of salvation in Christ!

We also felt the need to update the statistics and illustrations in the book. Trends among Christians worldwide since the early 1980s have greatly supported the key ideas in *Power Evangelism*.

Some readers will notice that we have dropped some material from the first edition. We did this because we were not satisfied with *how* we communicated our thoughts. For example, we completely dropped a section in which we compared power evangelism with programmatic evangelism. In the first edition we left the reader with the impression that we were criticising programmatic evangelism in its entirety. In fact, we believe in programmatic evangelism and practise it – as the Study Guide in this edition illustrates.

We also dropped the chapters in which we explored the three waves of the Holy Spirit in this century. We have written extensively about these issues elsewhere, and the Third Wave is now an accepted historical fact for most Christians – even for those who disagree with what it stands for.

Finally, in response to some valid criticism, we have added several new sections or further developed some of our key points. For example, you will notice a greater emphasis on the centrality of the cross in the proclamation of the gospel. And we have included a more detailed discussion of the cessationist theory of spiritual gifts (see Appendix C).

All of these changes mean the new edition is an improved

version of what was published back in 1985. This is truly a new book. Our prayers are that through reading it you will experience a renewed desire to spread the gospel.

JOHN WIMBER
KEVIN SPRINGER
Yorba Linda, California
January 1992

HOW TO USE THE STUDY GUIDE

Effective personal evangelism is not the product of happenstance. It requires understanding, good examples and personal practice for success. In other words, evangelism is a learned art.

When Jesus first called the disciples he said, 'Come, follow me, and I will make you fishers of men' (Matt. 4:19). Successful fishermen are careful planners. Their actions are premeditated, based on careful study, experience, and the answers to simple questions:

- What kind of fish are we going for? This determines where they will fish and the type of bait.
- What size of fish will we catch? This determines the strength of fishing line they need.
- What licence is required? Illegally caught fish cannot be kept.
- Where are we going to fish? Successful fishermen rely on accurate maps and experienced guides to find the best spots.

There's nothing haphazard about successful fishing. It's the same for fruitful evangelism. We need to know about the kind of people we are reaching out to, the most appropriate way to speak to them, our spiritual authority, and divine guidance. The Study Guide will help you grow in all of these areas.

Jesus also compared evangelism to farming (Matt. 13:3–43). Farmers work with different types of seeds and soils, fertilisers and irrigation methods. They must pay close attention to the weather, planting and harvesting at just the right time. And they must be patient, acknowledging their dependence on time and God's grace for fruitfulness.

The wise farmer leaves little to chance, and the wise Christian should do the same when spreading the seed of the kingdom of God in the world. My purpose, then, is to equip you to be effective fishers of men and women, to be wise harvesters of souls.

* * *

At the end of each section of this book you will find a project designed for small groups, though inspired and eager individuals will be able to adapt the material for personal study. I have a variety of small groups in mind: Sunday school classes, interdenominational Bible studies, fellowship gatherings, charismatic prayer groups, and church service teams.

I have several objectives for small groups that use the Study Guide. First, it is an aid for individual study, helping to highlight key issues raised in *Power Evangelism* and to stimulate thought and prayer. Second, it is a guide to group discussion and group exercises concerning key issues raised in the book. A by-product of this discussion is the inspiration and motivation to power evangelism. Third, it is a manual from which participants may learn how to lead others to faith in Christ.

To achieve these three objectives I have developed seven sessions, corresponding to the book's seven sections. The purpose statements at the beginning of each session inform the participant about what he or she should expect to learn. Pay close attention to these statements; I have worded them carefully. Usually the objective has two parts: gaining understanding about some topic (such as divine appointments or worldviews) and learning a new skill (such as how to break the ice in conversation with a stranger).

The seven sessions are most effectively covered at weekly intervals. This allows enough time to read and meditate on the four or five short chapters in each of the book's sections. More frequent gatherings will deny crucial individual study, prayer, and practice time; less frequent meetings will frustrate and discourage those eager to share their faith with others.

I recommend that the meetings always begin in worship and prayer. A by-product of worship is a learning environment, open hearts to the Holy Spirit, and faith for sharing the gospel. It is neither my place nor my desire to dictate a particular style of worship for your group; that is best determined by your particular tradition. God sees and recognises the attitude of your heart, that inner disposition of surrender and thanksgiving that may be expressed in exuberant singing, contemplative prayer, faithful liturgy. Usually small-group prayer and worship works well when a trained musician (a guitar- or piano-player) leads the groups in singing. Regardless of your worship style, we encourage you to invite the Holy Spirit to come among you, teach you, and release his love and power in you during the gathering.

The second part of the meeting is usually discussion, which in the first few meetings is based on the questions provided in the Study Guide. Later the discussion will focus on your experience in personal evangelism. As we wrote the questions we kept in mind a Persian proverb: 'It is harder to ask a sensible question than to supply a sensible answer.' We think 'sensible questions' for the purposes of small groups are discussion *starters* only, and they are intended to elicit other questions related to each topic. Many questions will point participants back to the book, forcing them to reread key sections carefully.

The key ingredient to a successful discussion is a gifted leader, a person who brings out the best in others without dominating the discussion. I do not believe the leader must be a great teacher or a fully matured evangelist with all the answers. Another factor in successful discussions is for each participant to review the questions before each session so that he or she can contribute thoughtful insights.

The last part of the meeting is prayer to put into action during the week what has been discussed. The most important quality for a successful small group is the willingness of participants to take risks, to step out in faith and reliance on the Spirit's leading and talk to people about Christ.

For many people personal evangelism is quite threatening, even frightening. Do not be alarmed by this. If you come with an open heart and a willingness to take some risks, you will experience some success. All of this takes time. Throughout the seven sessions you will grow in confidence, and many of you will see friends and family members come to a saving faith in Christ.

My hope is that this Study Guide will inspire you to spread the gospel. If as a result of this study only one person is saved because of you, it will have fulfilled our purpose.

PART ONE

The Kingdom Has Come

1

A POWERFUL EXPERIENCE

In the summer of 1967 a friend of mine, Scott (not his real name), attended a students' retreat at Arrowhead Springs, California, the headquarters of Campus Crusade for Christ International. A nineteen-year-old UCLA student, he had been a committed Christian for five years, but his spiritual life had recently stalled. He was looking for more from God, something to empower his life and give him a clearer purpose.

Arrowhead Springs is carved into the mountains overlooking the city of San Bernardino. During an earlier era it was an old health spa frequented by Hollywood stars; Greta Garbo and Clark Gable were reported to have sought 'the cure' in sulphur-laced, steamy caverns deep below the main hotel. Perhaps, Scott thought, he would find a spiritual cure during this week-long conference.

On arriving he discovered that he was to sleep in the hotel basement on a makeshift cot. Over seven hundred students from the United States and Canada jammed the facilities; it was not to be a Hollywood holiday. But that suited him well. It created an atmosphere of excitement and expectancy; if all these students had come from hundreds and even thousands of miles away, surely God would show up!

The theme of the conference was personal evangelism. Towards the end of the week the students were to be transported on buses to local beaches where, going two by

two, they would put into action what they had been taught –
they would evangelise complete strangers.

Scott was apprehensive about going out, especially since
he had been raised on the beaches of southern California
and was fearful of embarrassing encounters with old surfing
friends. Also, the idea of confronting complete strangers
with a planned presentation became more frightening as
the week progressed. At least, he soon discovered, they
were not going to his home beach.

The evening before they went out, Dr William Bright,
president of Campus Crusade, presented a teaching session
about the Holy Spirit. His points were very simple: we
cannot successfully live the Christian life in our own
strength; the Father has sent the Holy Spirit to empower
us; we are commanded in Scripture to 'be filled with the
Holy Spirit'.

For years Scott had been taught not to focus on the Holy
Spirit lest he weaken his relationship with Christ or fall into
the excesses of the Pentecostals. This could be dangerous,
leading possibly to deceit by the devil, even speaking in
tongues. Besides, he had heard many times, our primary
purpose should be fulfilling the great commission. An
emphasis on the Holy Spirit might distract us from this
important task.

But Dr Bright's talk stirred Scott deeply, allaying many
of his fears. Dr Bright said that only through the power of
the Holy Spirit could we fulfil the great commission. (It was
one of the few positive teaching sessions Scott had ever
heard on the Third Person of the Trinity.) 'Perhaps,' Scott
mused, 'this is the key to the refreshing I seek.'

That night Scott could hardly sleep, intermittently wak-
ing and thinking about Dr Bright's words. By one o'clock
he was wide-eyed, staring at the tangle of pipes and electri-
cal tubing overhead, sensing God calling him to open his
heart fully to the Holy Spirit. So he slipped out of bed,
dressed, and found a quiet place under a lonely palm tree in
the hotel grounds, near an illuminated swimming pool.

Unsure of what to expect, his hunger for God motivated

him to pray. 'Holy Spirit,' he pleaded, 'I have been living in my own strength too long. Now I yield every part of my life to you. Come and fill me.'

What happened next was beyond anything Scott had been taught about how God works. First, he felt a rush of power come over his body, a warm, tingling feeling he had never before experienced. With that rush came a peace and an urge to worship God. As he began worshipping he was soon speaking in tongues, though initially he was unsure of what it was. After praying and worshipping for an hour, he opened his Bible and began reading . . . and reading . . . and reading – late into the night. Scripture came alive; the very word of God leaped off the pages.

The next day, knowing staff members were not sympathetic to charismatic phenomena, he told no one of his experience. 'Was it real?' he wondered. It had to be. He was a different person, though confused about the meaning of what had happened. As the time to go to the beaches approached, he noticed the gospel burned in his heart, pressing every part of his being with an urgency to tell others about Jesus Christ.

Scott boarded the bus without any fear, though he was still not looking forward to talking with strangers. But now he sensed his experience the night before would help him on the beaches.

His partner, Jim, a student at the University of North Carolina, was apprehensive. Scott knew that the Holy Spirit was telling him to take the lead on the beach. He prayed quietly as the bus snaked its way across the freeways leading to Newport Beach.

Newport Beach is typical of many beaches in southern California – sand covered with thousands of young people flocked around blasting radios, sharing the latest gossip, telling jokes, and watching other boys and girls walk by. Out into this mass of oily, tanning flesh went the God squads.

Scott and Jim first approached two Hispanic teenage boys, asking if they would mind participating in a religious survey (the survey was part of the evangelism programme, a way of beginning conversation with strangers). Soon they were talking about Jesus Christ. Two girls joined the conversation, then another three boys. Scott was telling the teenagers about their sins and God's grace. As he spoke he received insights about the teenagers – sexual sins, problems with parents, problems at school – that were right on target. Supernaturally knowing what their greatest needs were, he spoke with authority about God's love and righteousness in a way that opened their hearts. Jim stood by, astonished.

Within thirty minutes several of the teenagers were weeping, falling to their knees, repenting of their sins, and turning to Christ. Before the day was over at least a dozen young people made Christian commitments. In several instances students who initially joined the conversation only to mock and ridicule Scott ended up on their faces, weeping, trembling, and repenting.

Scott proclaimed the gospel with uncommon authority. His words and actions were so persuasive that a group of antagonistic teenagers from a different culture were converted in mass. There was *power* in his proclamation and demonstration. Later in the book I will take a much closer look at how his supernatural insights into their lives affected his witness. But first, in the remainder of this section, I will introduce you to the ultimate source of 'power' in power evangelism: the kingdom of God.

2

THE KINGDOM OF GOD

Scott preached good news to his teenage audience, that God has provided forgiveness of sins and eternal life through the life, death and resurrection of Jesus Christ (1 Cor. 15:3–8). The gospel itself, Paul said, 'is the power of God for the salvation of everyone who believes' (Rom. 1:16). But how could a message contain such power? The answer lies in what salvation means: the coming of the kingdom of God.

The good news Jesus proclaimed was the gospel of the kingdom of God. 'The time has come,' Mark summarises Jesus as preaching at the beginning of his public ministry. 'The kingdom of God is near. Repent and believe the good news!' (Mark 1:15). Thus the heart of Jesus' message was both the proclamation of God's action – 'The kingdom . . . is near' – and the demand for a response from all who heard – 'Repent and believe . . .'

Jesus was telling his Jewish audience that his Father's promise to their father, Abraham, was about to be fulfilled:

> 'I will make you into a great nation
>   and I will bless you;
> I will make your name great,
>   and you will be a blessing.
> I will bless those who bless you,
>   and whoever curses you I will curse;
> and all peoples on earth
>   will be blessed through you.' (Gen. 12:2–3)

Jesus was proclaiming nothing less than the hope of Israel's salvation, that God was coming to redeem and bless them and establish his reign over all the earth. This salvation was summed up in the idea that 'the kingdom of God' was close. For the duration of his public ministry, Jesus demonstrated that the kingdom of God was near by healing the sick, casting out demons, and raising the dead. Every miraculous act had a purpose: to confront people with his message that *in him* the kingdom had come, and that they had to decide to accept or reject it.

Despite different ideas about what the hope of salvation would look like (there were in Christ's day many interpretations), all Jews eagerly anticipated a day of salvation, a time of fulfilment. But what did the 'kingdom of God' mean to Jesus and his listeners? From where did the term come? Through the parables and their interpretations (usually given privately to the disciples), Christ transformed what was commonly accepted about the kingdom of God in his day.

Most first-century Jews held one of two popular understandings about the kingdom of God. The first came from the Old Testament prophets. They taught a day was coming ('the Day of the Lord') when God would come and restore his people, Israel, as a unified political and geographical entity. Salvation meant the return of a single, strong Jewish nation, as in the days of King David (see Isa. 11). It was not a spiritual and other-worldly kingdom; it was the dream of Jewish nationalism. This appears to be what the Jews in general were looking for at the time of Christ, and how they understood him when he spoke of the kingdom. John 6:15 clearly supports this. The people wanted to make Jesus king of Israel by force. Even the disciples, after being with him for years, longed for the restoration of Israel (Acts 1:6).

This was not the only popularly accepted understanding of the kingdom of God in Christ's day. During the inter-testamental period (approximately 200 BC to the New Testament era), the time in which the apocalyptic literature was written, the term 'kingdom of God' came into widespread usage. The apocalyptic writers foresaw an end to the present age, after which God would create a new world in which all evil, demons, sickness and death would be defeated.[1]

Jesus in part held both of these views. He used Old Testament and intertestamental terms like the 'kingdom of God' and 'ages', building on and transforming their popularly accepted meanings, to explain why he came. For example, in explaining the parable of the wheat and the weeds, Jesus used terms like 'the sons of the kingdom', 'the sons of the evil one', 'the end of the age', and 'the righteous will shine like the sun in the kingdom of their Father' (Matt. 13:36–43; see also 1 Cor. 2:6; Gal. 1:4). He taught the disciples that, like the Old Testament prophets, he too saw an imminent day of judgement for the nations, the Son of Man being the Judge. And like the apocalyptic writers, he too foresaw a sudden end to the present age, and its replacement by a future age – 'the kingdom of [the] Father'.

George Ladd summarises scriptural teaching on the two ages with these words:

> In brief, this age, which extends from creation to the Day of the Lord . . . is the age of human existence in weakness and mortality, of evil, sin, and death. The Age to Come will see the realization of all that the reign of God means, and will be the age of resurrection into eternal life in the Kingdom of God. Everything in the Gospels points to the idea that life in the Kingdom of God in the Age to Come will be life on the earth – but life transformed by the kingly rule of God when his people enter into the full measure of the divine blessings (Mt. 19:28).[2]

The following diagram, adapted from Ladd's work,[3] helps us visualise the present and future aspects of the kingdom of God:

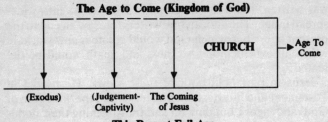

It was with this understanding that John the Baptist made his announcement: 'Repent, for the kingdom of heaven is near' (Matt. 3:2). God was ready to bring the new age into existence. John announced the new age would soon be here. Later Jesus said, '. . . the kingdom of God has come upon you' (Matt. 12:28). But in what way could the kingdom be upon them?

3

CAUGHT BETWEEN TWO AGES

To understand how Jesus could embody the kingdom of God, we must take a closer look at the meaning of the word 'kingdom'.[1] In the New Testament, the Greek word *basileia* means 'kingship' or 'royal rule'. It is normally translated 'kingdom'. It implies exercise of kingly rule or reign rather than simply a geographic realm over which a king rules. Westerners conceive of kingdoms largely in terms of realms. For example, the United Kingdom conjures up thoughts of the territory encompassing British lands. The biblical concept goes beyond the idea of a realm to emphasise dynamic rule.

When Jesus said that the kingdom or rulership of God had come *in him*, he meant that God had come to claim what was rightfully his. The future age, the kingdom of God, invaded the present age, the realm of Satan.[2] Jesus did not consign the kingdom of God to a future millennium. When he said that the kingdom of God had come in him, he claimed for himself the position of a divine invader, coming to set everything straight: 'The reason the Son of God appeared was to destroy the devil's work' (1 John 3:8).

This explains the twofold pattern of Christ's ministry, repeated wherever he went: first *proclamation*, then *demonstration*. First he preached repentance and the good news of the kingdom of God. Then he cast out demons, healed the sick, raised the dead – which proved he was the presence of the kingdom, the Anointed One.

Jesus came as a Jew to Israel. He accepted the authority

of the Old Testament and basically ministered to the 'lost sheep of Israel' (Matt. 10:5–7). He offered kingdom rule to the Jews first, but they rejected it. Jesus was grieved (Matt. 23:37–9). However, while Israel *as a nation* rejected Christ, a remnant did accept him, and these few were the foundation of the New Testament Church (Rom. 11:1–24). In the New Testament, the Church enters into the covenant blessings of Israel.[3]

*   *   *

Some Christians, unclear about the relationship between the kingdom of God and the Church,[4] confuse the two and teach that the Church *is* the kingdom. This leads to serious error, such as equating church membership with final salvation. The Church is an avenue to salvation, in so far as it leads people to union with Christ, but the Church is not the source of salvation.

The kingdom of God created the Church at Pentecost through the outpouring of the Holy Spirit. The Church is the primary (though not the exclusive) residence of God's dynamic rule. This means the Church witnesses to the King and his kingdom, but it does not have authority in itself to build the kingdom. Only God has that authority.

When the Church is confused with the kingdom, leaders assume that God's authority is coextensive with the office they hold, that *they* are the rule of God. Authoritarianism and even cultishness can be an unfortunate result of this kind of thinking. When pastoral leaders understand that their authority is derived from the kingdom of God, and that rule is not equated with office, they are restrained from leading in their own authority.

The Church is also the instrument of the kingdom. The disciples not only proclaimed the King and his kingdom, they also demonstrated the works and miracles of the kingdom. Jesus told Peter that 'the gates of Hades will not overcome [the Church]' (Matt. 16:18). The 'gates of Hades' are the strongholds of evil and death, satanic powers that seek to destroy us (Eph. 6:10–12). As Christ's instruments, we wage war against these strongholds, replacing their dominion with the kingdom of God.

With this in mind, Christ commissioned the Twelve (Matt. 10:5–16), the Seventy-two (Luke 10:1–20), and now commissions us (Matt. 28:18–20). During the forty days between his resurrection and his ascension, Jesus spoke to the apostles about the kingdom of God (Acts 1:3). In Samaria, Philip 'preached the good news of the kingdom of God' (Acts 8:12), and Peter, James and Paul all mention the kingdom of God in their letters.

When Scott went out on the beach and preached the gospel of the King and his kingdom, and demonstrated God's presence through supernatural insights into the teenagers' lives, he ushered in God's rule and authority. It was a confrontation between two worlds – Satan's and God's – and God won.

I believe the most effective form of evangelism today has at its heart the proclamation of the King and his kingdom. We'll take a closer look at the gospel of the kingdom in the next chapter.

4

THE GOSPEL OF THE KINGDOM

Proclamation of a faulty gospel will produce faulty or, at best, weak Christians. Such is the case all too often today. Instead of a call to the King and his kingdom, people are hearing a gospel that emphasises self: come to Jesus and get this or that need met, be personally fulfilled, reach your potential. This, however, is not the costly kingdom gospel that Christ proclaims: 'I am the resurrection and the life. He who believes in me will live, even though he dies' (John 11:25).

The gospel of the kingdom is costly because it cost God *everything* – the death of his Son on the cross. Jesus' death on the cross is central to everything he accomplished, for it removed the barrier of sin that separates men and women from God. Out of God's love for us, he sacrificed his Son so we could have eternal life. 'For God so loved the world', John 3:16 says, 'that he gave his one and only Son . . .'

For us to gain eternal life, Jesus *had* to die to satisfy God's justice. It may be difficult to think of the God of love as a God of wrath, but Scripture tells us this is so (Rom. 1:18). So the cross makes it possible for God simultaneously to take our sin seriously and to extend his love to us. God's justice demands our death as punishment for our sin, yet his love desires that we be saved from the judgement of hell. At the cross God 'demonstrate[d] his justice at the present time, so as to be just and the one who justifies those who have faith in Jesus' (Rom. 3:26). God's love cannot operate apart from the cross, for forgiveness cannot come except through the cross.

Two terms capture how much the cross cost God. The first is *atonement*. Hebrews 2:17 says that Jesus came 'that he might make atonement for the sins of the people'. The word 'atonement' means 'a making at one'. It points to the process by which God brings us into union with himself. The atonement makes us one with God through turning aside God's wrath and making him favourably inclined towards us. The key to God's turning aside is that Christ uniquely takes our place (he is our substitute, John 11:50; 1 Tim. 2:6), enduring God's wrath for us. Jesus also represents us on the cross (2 Cor. 5:14), so that as we identify with him, the benefits of his death are applied to us.

To first-century Jewish Christians 'atonement' brought to mind the bloody sacrificial rites of the Old Testament. When Christ was said to atone for our sins, they thought of him as a blood sacrifice that removes sin. When it is said that Jesus died 'on behalf of' human beings, or when Hebrews 7:27 describes Jesus as a high priest sacrificing himself, this is the language of atonement. The concept is that instead of a sinner dying for his or her own sins, a substitute (normally an animal) is offered and dies in his or her place. The blood poured out represents the life that has been sacrificed and becomes a symbol of all the benefits of the sacrifice.

The second term that captures the cost of the cross is *justification*. Justification is a legal term meaning 'to acquit' or 'to declare righteous'. It is the opposite of condemnation. Justification refers to God's righteousness being credited to us. Paul says, 'Consider Abraham: "He believed God, and it was credited to him as righteousness"' (Gal. 3:6). Elsewhere he says, 'God made him [Jesus] who had no sin to be sin for us, so that in him we might become the righteousness of God' (2 Cor. 5:21). When we put our faith in Christ (see Acts 10:43) we become so closely identified with him that his righteousness is credited to us, and we are declared righteous.

This is because, rather than looking at our deeds, which are evil, God, when he looks at us, sees the blood. Romans

5:9 says that we have been 'justified by his [Jesus'] blood'. In Romans 6:1–10, Paul says God can declare us righteous because, through faith in Christ, we have died to sin. 'Anyone who has died', he argues in Romans 6:7, 'has been freed from sin.' The Greek word translated 'freed' in this verse is the word for 'justified'. If by faith we identify with Christ's sacrifice on the cross, we are justified from sin and declared righteous.

God paid the high cost for making eternal life available to us. But what's our part? How do we enter an eternal relationship with God? We enter through faith in Christ: 'Believe in the Lord Jesus Christ, and you will be saved' (Acts 16:31). It cost God everything, and there is *nothing* that we can do to receive it – except believe. And even belief, Paul says, is ultimately a gift of God (Eph. 2:8). No amount of effort or good intentions will get us one inch closer to heaven.

*   *   *

None of this is to imply, however, that the Christian life is a bowl of cherries. Once we place our trust in Christ, we are drafted into a fierce spiritual battle. Often kingdom life is likened to a Caribbean cruise on a luxury liner. People change into their leisure clothes, grab their suntan lotion, and saunter down to the docks. What a shock it is when they find that living in the kingdom is really more like enlisting in the navy and doing battle with a vicious enemy.

For example, the enemy follows no rules of war. Satan considers nothing unfair; he is not a gentleman. The sooner Christians understand this, the more serious they will become about being equipped and properly trained for the kingdom.

Although he follows no rules, we know Satan attacks on three fronts: through the flesh, through the world, and by direct assault. Because a major concern of this book is warfare against the direct assaults of Satan, I will only make a few comments on the first two, devoting the remainder of the section to the latter.[1]

The flesh. In the 1936 Spanish Civil War, Franco's Loyalist Army defeated the Republican Army in Madrid. It was the key battle of the war and led to the establishment of Franco's government in Spain. When asked what was the key to his victory, Franco replied, 'the fifth column'. He had four columns of troops engaged openly, and a 'fifth column' of loyalists *inside* Madrid who, through sabotage, seriously weakened the Republican Army.

We too contend against a fifth column, 'sinful passions' that reside in us. In Paul's words, 'I know that nothing good lives in me, that is, in my sinful nature' (Rom. 7:18). The enemy loves to exploit and excite our 'fifth column' – the sin that dwells in our flesh – through temptation. But God has given us the power to walk by faith and resist that temptation.

The world. Psalm 137:4 says, 'How can we sing the songs of the Lord while in a foreign land?' How can Christians serve God's kingdom while taking on the values and lifestyles of the world? We cannot.

When we think of ourselves as an army, the issue of discipline and the fulfilment of kingdom standards becomes more critical than personal security and ease. Sometimes a Christian soldier looks at civilian life and says, 'That lifestyle looks attractive. I like the glitter of materialism, the thrill of personal power, the pleasure of sexual immorality, the quest for self-fulfilment. That life sure beats this one.' When that happens, discipline is lost, and we are infiltrated and eventually taken captive. Paul has strong advice about this: 'No-one serving as a soldier gets involved in civilian affairs – he wants to please his commanding officer' (2 Tim. 2:4).

We have been given the keys to the kingdom, the authority and power over the enemy, but if we do not exercise that power, it is of no use. The kingdom of darkness is organised to distract us, to prevent us from doing God's bidding. Through the glitter of materialism and power, sexual immorality, and the promise of self-fulfilment, Satan diverts our attention from the kingdom of God.

Fellowship with other Christians in local churches – outposts of the kingdom – is a primary defence against being taken in by the world. Prayer, Bible study and spiritual disciplines such as fasting are necessary not only to gain God's power and insight but also to equip us to resist the world.

The devil. In John 10:10 we read that Satan has well-defined objectives: 'The thief comes only to steal and kill and destroy . . .' We also observe that it is the devil and his demons, not men and women, against whom we war (Eph. 6:12).

Our situation is similar to that of an underground army living in a land still occupied by a defeated enemy. Such was the French underground's role after D-Day during the Second World War. Though their eventual defeat was certain, the Germans were still capable of committing atrocities on French civilians. The 1984 arrest and trial of Klaus Barbie illustrates how barbarous the Germans' acts were: knowing there was no hope for German victory, Barbie nevertheless tortured and murdered hundreds of French – including children. He was nicknamed 'the Butcher of Lyon'.

Satan has many names too: Destroyer, Deceiver, Liar – the Butcher of the World. In our war with Satan there are no demilitarised zones. There is never a lull in the fighting. We are born into the fight, and – unless the Day of the Lord comes – we will die in the fight. We should never expect the battle to cease.

The kingdom of Satan was and is Christ's real enemy, and there is a war going on. Jesus is about his Father's business, which is releasing those held captive by Satan. The final outcome of the battle has been assured through Christ's death, resurrection and ascension to the place of all authority, the right hand of the Father (1 Cor. 15:20–8). But Satan is not yet cast out, and he will not be until Christ returns to establish his kingdom for ever. So we are caught between two ages. The fight continues, and we are in it.

5

POWER AND AUTHORITY

To fight effectively, we must correctly understand power
and authority in the kingdom. In Luke 9:1–2 we read:
'When Jesus had called the Twelve together, *he gave them
power and authority* to drive out all demons and to cure
diseases, and he sent them out to preach the kingdom of
God and to heal the sick.' He gave them power and
authority to cure diseases and drive out *all* demons. According to Acts 1:8, power was to come from the Holy
Spirit. Power is the ability, the strength, the might to
complete a given task. Authority is the right to use the
power of God.

For example, a traffic policeman does not have the
physical power to stop cars. However, he does stop them,
because he wears a badge and a uniform given him by a
higher authority. We have been given a badge and a
uniform by Jesus. These gifts become effective when we
learn to wear and use them correctly.

In Scripture, the centurion understood how authority
and power work (Matt. 8:5–13). He was a man both under
the authority of some and having authority over others. He
knew how to receive and give orders. After asking Jesus to
heal his paralysed servant – to which Jesus responded that
he would 'go and heal him' – the centurion replied: 'Just say
the word, and my servant will be healed.' Jesus, 'astonished' by the centurion's words, said, 'I have not found
anyone in Israel with such great faith.'

*   *   *

Our difficulty is that we have not learned to receive or give orders. To a great extent, we practise a cosmetic Christianity, because we misunderstand our initial call to Christ. We think that the key to maturity and power is to be 'good'. We then focus on our behaviour. But our behaviour never meets the high standards of Christ's righteousness.

I did this for years. By focusing on my behaviour, I was in constant turmoil, because my behaviour was never good enough, rarely meeting God's (or my own) standards of righteousness. I first believed in Christ because I was not good, yet after becoming a Christian I still struggled in my own strength with not being good enough. So I was always under conviction, always struggling with guilt.

Then one day, twenty-two years ago, I fell to my knees and asked God to help me. I sensed him respond, 'Since you can do nothing without me, how much help do you want?' Then he said, 'The issue is not being good, it is being God's. Just come to me, and I'll provide goodness for you.'

I did not fully understand his words. What did he mean, 'I'll provide goodness for you'? I was confused, so for the next five years I tried to be good in my own strength. I soon became more and more despondent. Finally, I began to ask God about what I sensed he had told me earlier concerning his goodness. He explained that he had good works prepared for me, but they were *his* works, and *I* could not do them for him. He told me that I needed to begin to listen to his voice rather than try to distil the Christian life down to a set of rules and principles. I began to listen more during my times of prayer and Bible study, and more consciously talked with him throughout the normal activities of the day.

Then something interesting began to happen. He put new desires and attitudes in me. His Spirit began to strengthen me to do righteous acts I previously had no desire for. I began to sense his voice more often throughout the day. And good works were multiplied in my life.

Today I no longer try to be good; instead, I am only concerned with doing God's bidding: what he commands, I do. Now my personal life is more conformed to his righteousness and character than it used to be. Following his commands does not leave much time for sin.

Most of us are confused about how to live a life of faith. We cannot understand or relate to the enormous efforts it took to do the things that Jesus did. The reason is that too often we are searching for methods, formulas and principles that will open the power of God to us, becoming frustrated each time we try another 'key' that does not work.

Again, *we* are not the kingdom; we are instruments of the kingdom. The works of the kingdom are performed through us; thus our purpose is to witness about what God has done, is doing, and will do. Like Jesus, we have come to do the will of the Father. When asked how we should pray, Jesus taught us, 'Our Father in heaven . . . your kingdom come, your will be done on earth as it is in heaven' (Matt. 6:9–10). As the centurion did, we must learn how to hear and believe Jesus' commands if we expect to be the vehicles of signs and miracles for the kingdom.

*   *   *

In *The Real Satan* James Kallas says:

> A war is going on! Cosmic war! Jesus is the divine invader sent by God to shatter the strengths of Satan. In that light, the whole ministry of Jesus unrolls. Jesus has one purpose – to defeat Satan. He takes seriously the strength of the enemy.[1]

Kallas' remarks raise a significant question: Who is attacking the territory of the other, Christ or Satan, and what difference does the answer to this question make to Christians? The difference affects our attitude and stance towards the Christian life. If Jesus is the invader, Satan is consigned to the defensive. We become offensive soldiers, taking territory and redeeming lives – we are Christ's co-belligerents.

Jesus says the same thing in Matthew 11:12: 'From the days of John the Baptist until now, the kingdom of heaven has been forcefully advancing, and forceful men lay hold of it.' George Ladd points out that this verse may be interpreted several ways, depending on how the Greek term for 'forcefully advancing' is translated. It may be understood as 'to exercise force' or as 'to be treated forcibly'. The latter translation implies that Satan wars directly on the kingdom of God, putting Christ and us on the defensive.

But Ladd argues that 'we do not discover [in the New Testament] the idea of Satan attacking the kingdom of God or exercising his power against the kingdom itself. *He can only wage his war against the sons of the kingdom . . . God is the aggressor; Satan is on the defensive*' (emphasis mine).[2] Ladd concludes that the best option is that 'the kingdom of heaven "exercises its force" or "makes its way powerfully" in the world'.[3] *We* are thrust into the middle of a battle with Satan: it's a tug-of-war, and the prize is the souls of men and women. Satan's captivity of men and women has many facets, but denying them final salvation is his primary goal. But there are other types of dominion: bondage to sin, physical and emotional problems, social disruption, and demonic affliction.

Our mission is to rescue those who have been taken captive as a result of Adam's fall. How we fulfil our mission is what the remainder of this book is about.

Study Session 1

THE KINGDOM OF GOD

Read *Power Evangelism*, Part One, chapters 1–5.

Purpose

Many Christians give little thought to the kingdom of God, unaware that it was the focus of Jesus' preaching and teaching. Yet the kingdom of God is a power point for personal evangelism. Unless we are kingdom people, there will be very little power in our witness. In this session you will explore how the kingdom of God affects you personally.

Introduction

The goal of the discussion session is to introduce the participants to the book *Power Evangelism* and the structure of the seven-week group study sessions, and to take time to answer the discussion questions.

After a period of worship and prayer, take five minutes to review individually the questions below. The purpose of these questions is not to harmonise your answers with the book's teaching; it is to help you form an opinion about the kingdom of God as it affects your life. So be prepared to discuss your answers.

Personal Project

Answer the following questions by circling 'Yes', 'No', or 'Sometimes'.

1. I have had an experience in personal evangelism similar to Scott's in chapter 1.   Yes   No   Sometimes

2. Before reading this section of *Power Evangelism* I was aware of the centrality of the kingdom of God in Jesus' teaching and preaching.   Yes   No   Sometimes

3. I understand that evangelism involves proclaiming and demonstrating the gospel of the kingdom of God.   Yes   No   Sometimes

4. In my witnessing I talk about the King and his kingdom.   Yes   No   Sometimes

5. Almost daily I have experiences in which I become aware that my ethical standards conflict with those of most people around me.   Yes   No   Sometimes

6. It isn't unusual for someone to ask me, 'What's so different about you?'   Yes   No   Sometimes

7. People regularly ask me about my relationship with God.   Yes   No   Sometimes

8. I am a generous financial giver to my church.   Yes   No   Sometimes

9. I have no problem respecting and supporting the leaders in my congregation.
   Yes   No   Sometimes

10. There are significant areas of my life that I have not allowed God's rule into.
    Yes   No   Sometimes

11. My prayer life is marked by submission and intimacy with God to such an extent that there are few moments during the day in which I am not aware of God's presence and my dependence on him.
    Yes   No   Sometimes

12. I feel like I have missed out on a significant source of strength and direction when I cannot participate in Sunday worship.
    Yes   No   Sometimes

13. Overall my lifestyle conforms to what I believe.
    Yes   No   Sometimes

14. I regularly talk with others about their relationship with God.
    Yes   No   Sometimes

15. My relationships with other Christians are sources of strength that make me a more effective witness for Jesus Christ.
    Yes   No   Sometimes

16. God regularly directs me to talk to people about Jesus.
    Yes   No   Sometimes

Further Discussion

The goal of the discussion session is to assess what you
believe about the King and the kingdom of God, to increase your understanding about the kingdom of God, and
to encourage you to allow the King to have greater influence on how you live.

The leader will guide the group through the above
questions in open discussion.

Plan of Action

Each participant should make a list of five people they
know and whom they would like to talk to about the
kingdom of God. Pray for them daily, and ask God for the
opportunity to talk to *one* of them this week.

1.

2.

3.

4.

5.

For Next Week

Come prepared to share your evangelistic experience with
the group.

Read *Power Evangelism*, Part Two, chapters 6–9.

PART TWO

The Power Encounter

6

THE FIGHT

I was woken late one night in 1978 by a desperate phone call. 'Please, Pastor Wimber, come and help Melinda!' a young man cried into the telephone. He went on to explain that his friend Melinda (not her real name) was in a pick-up truck in a nearby field. Although she was only eighteen years old and weighed only a hundred pounds, she was thrashing about so violently that the truck was rocking. Strange, growling, animal-like sounds were coming from her – not her normal voice at all.

I was to meet a demon.

Before this I had believed in the existence of demons and had probably even met a few without knowing it, but this was the first time I met one who was openly manifesting all of its evil, lying and foul deeds through another human being. This was a pastoral call that I would never forget.

After I arrived at the garage from which the boy had phoned me, he took me to the truck. The girl, or rather something in the girl, spoke. 'I know you' were the first words to assault me – packaged in a hoarse, eerie voice – 'and you don't know what you're doing.'

I thought, 'You're right.'

The demon then said through Melinda, 'You can't do anything with her. She's mine.'

I thought, 'You're wrong.' I knew little to nothing about how to cast out demons, but I also knew the New Testament taught that I had *some* authority and responsibility to deal with them.

Then began ten hours of spiritual warfare during which I called on the forces of heaven to overcome Satan. I thumbed through the Gospels, looking for passages on the casting out of demons. During this time I smelled putrid odours from the girl and saw her eyes roll back and her profuse perspiration. I heard blasphemy and saw wild physical activity that required more strength than a slight girl operating under her own power could possibly possess. I was appalled and very afraid, but I refused to give up the fight.

In the end I think the demon left because I wore it out, certainly not because I was skilled at casting out evil spirits. (Since that time I have learned much about this type of encounter. If I had known then what I know now, I am convinced the episode would not have taken longer than an hour.)[1]

*   *   *

Encounters with demons have become a common experience for me. Alan Tippett calls these events *power encounters*, the clashing of the kingdom of God with the kingdom of Satan.[2] These conflicts, these clashes, may occur anywhere, any time. The expulsion of demons is most dramatic, though power encounters are far from limited only to those where Satan attacks through the demonic.

Any system or force that must be overcome for the gospel to be believed is cause for a power encounter. In each case, unbelief is the evil that is conquered in a power encounter. In fact, unbelief *is* the kingdom of Satan, albeit a far less visible form of him than demons or illness. When we experience the Holy Spirit and are able to convert unbelievers, we are the vehicles through which the kingdom of God defeats the kingdom of Satan. This is especially true in the area of missions. C. Peter Wagner, professor of church growth at Fuller Theological Seminary in Pasadena, California, commenting on power encounters and evangelism among tribal groups, writes that 'a power encounter is a visible, practical demonstration that Jesus Christ is more powerful than the false gods or spirits worshiped or feared by a people group'.[3] This results in the conversion of members of the tribal groups.

Jesus began his public ministry with a power encounter (Mark 1:21–34). Soon after his forty days of fasting and testing in the wilderness, he went throughout Galilee proclaiming the gospel and calling the first disciples. Eventually he arrived in Capernaum, where he attended a synagogue meeting. As was the tradition for visiting rabbis, Jesus taught the people. The people were 'amazed at his teaching, because he taught them as one who had authority, not as the teachers of the law'. A demon-possessed man cried out, 'What do you want with us, Jesus of Nazareth? Have you come to destroy us? I know who you are – the Holy One of God!'

Here was a clear challenge to the kingdom of God. How did Christ respond? He silenced the spirit, then called it out of the man. The people were impressed with his power: 'He even gives orders to evil spirits and they obey him.' That evening, in response to the morning's deliverance, a large crowd gathered near the place where he was staying, and he again drove out demons and 'healed many who had various diseases'.

Probably the most dramatic illustration of this type of encounter in the Old Testament is found in the story of Elijah confronting the four hundred and fifty prophets of Baal on Mount Carmel (1 Kings 18:16–45). Here we see God's prophet encountering an impotent god, a graven image representing a religious system that Satan backed.

After the wicked King Ahab accused Elijah of causing trouble in Israel, Elijah challenged him to an open confrontation: my God versus your Baal – and whoever is left standing at the end is the True God. Ahab accepted. Before all the people, the Lord overwhelmed Baal. During the confrontation Elijah taunted the false prophets about Baal's impotence: 'Shout louder! Surely he is a god! Perhaps he is deep in thought, or busy, or travelling. Maybe he is sleeping and must be awakened.' Elijah was aggressive, full of zeal for God's authority, seizing the opportunity not only to defeat Satan but also to demonstrate the lordship of the true God.

The key to the entire episode was Elijah's doing what God told him. He was a servant of God. 'O Lord, God of Abraham, Isaac, and Israel,' he prayed, 'let it be known today that you are God in Israel and that I am your servant and have done all these things *at your command*' (v. 36, emphasis mine). After this prayer, the fire of God fell, proving his presence. God's servant was vindicated. The response from the people was immediate: 'The Lord – he is God! The Lord – he is God!'

*   *   *

Primitive peoples often need to see the superior power of the gospel demonstrated for them to believe. C. Peter Wagner received this report from Terrie L. Lillie, a student who documented it in a village in Kenya. It is told by an eyewitness whose primary language is not English.

A child was deadly sick in the same house after the end of the second week. She had malaria and surely she was dying. We were awakened at night by a big cry. We all ran to the direction of my grandmother's house. Kavili was crying, and Mbulu and the old woman, Kanini, the child born recently, was dying. She had changed her color and her eyes had turned completely white. There was no blinking.

Many more people were there and a lot more were coming. I got inside. Here was the people who did not know what to do and how to do it. It was as they were in the middle of the night, with no car or anything which could help anyone. No medicine was available at that time. Something had to be done. I thought it would be a good idea to pray and see what we would do next.

I asked to be given the child. I put her under my arms and called my wife to come near. I told everyone to come in that we may pray for the dying child. They came in but some feared that the child was going to die and so they did not go inside the house with a dead child. Then I had all of them sit. I began to pray. I did not make a long prayer. I said very few words. I simply asked the Lord to heal the child in the name of Jesus. Then I gave the child back to the mother.

The moment I gave it back, she was well. She was now breathing. She began to cry, she was nursed and she was well. Everyone took time to praise the name of the Lord. I could not really understand what was happening but I felt the power of God proceed out of me, and for a moment I did not want to say a lot of things. This was a big issue which made everyone present wonder to see how the Lord worked so quickly.

As a result of this, the whole village became Christians.

In this instance, a fatal illness needed to be overcome to open up the villagers to faith in Christ.

*   *   *

Pradip Sudra, an Indian missionary from Great Britain, recently described an event in the southern Gujarat State that again illustrates the very human need to see the superior power of God actually demonstrated. In 1983 Pradip was on a mission with Operation Mobilisation. He was accompanied by a half dozen co-workers. Solid evangelicals, they were all fairly inexperienced in ministering with supernatural signs, wonders, and healings. Their custom was to go from village to village in a truck with large letters painted on it proclaiming, 'Jesus Saves and He's Alive.' The main road passed many small roads or mud trails that would lead back to a village. They would enter each side road to hand out tracts and do some preaching in one village after another.

The driver passed one side road without the slightest hesitation. Pradip sensed in his spirit that they should go up that road, and told the driver to turn around and go back.

The driver said, 'No, that's a Muslim village. If we go there, they'll stone us. They'll beat us.' Nevertheless, Pradip urged him to go back and turn in to the village. As the truck entered the village, it was quickly surrounded by a large group of hostile men and boys with clubs and stones.

Before any action started, the local Muslim Mullah (leader) came out and tried to calm down the crowd. He turned to the Christians and said, 'Hey, I've also heard that Jesus heals. Now if you are true servants of Jesus, then I want you to do one thing. I'll let you preach in this village, but only on one condition. That is, my wife has been ill. She's in bed. She's been there for five years. She has stomach cramps. Pray for her. If she gets healed you have my permission to preach here. If she doesn't get healed . . .' 'We knew what the results would be,' Pradip says. 'They'd really beat us.'

Pradip took one colleague with him and accompanied the Mullah to his cottage. They had the husband lay hands on her, for it was culturally inappropriate for them to do so. They then prayed that she would be released from the spirit that was oppressing her. Instantly she was healed and rose up. She served them some tea.

They were urged by the people to stay on, which they did for three weeks. Each morning and evening they taught the people Bible stories and songs about Jesus. At the end of three weeks the villagers said, 'There's a river just down the hill from here. We want to be baptised.' Two hundred and fifty people – virtually all the villagers above the age of twelve or thirteen – were baptised in one service.

A full-time pastor was sent out to the village from Tamil Nadu by an Indian mission called the Friends Missionary Prayer Band. Today the church is self-supporting and is sending out workers to share Jesus with their surrounding villages. Pradip Sudra has made occasional visits back to the village to verify the ongoing fruit of power evangelism.[4]

7

A WAR ZONE

An analogy that may help us understand what I mean by the term power encounter is found in nature. When warm and cold fronts collide, violence ensues: thunder and lightning, rain or snow – even tornadoes or hurricanes. There is conflict and a resulting release of energy. It is disorderly, messy, and difficult to control.

Power encounters are much like that. When the kingdom of God comes into direct contact with the kingdom of the world (when Jesus meets Satan), there is conflict. And usually it too is disorderly, messy, and difficult for us to control.

The greatest instance of this was the crucifixion of Christ. At that moment an eternal sacrifice was made for us, so that our sin might be forgiven and the flesh, the world and the devil might be utterly defeated. Great power was released that day. All of creation was rocked: the earth shook, rocks split, the sun stopped shining for three hours, and the Temple curtain was torn in two. Even tombs were opened, releasing the dead – 'holy people' (Matt. 27:52). Life was radiating from the death of Christ; it shook a creation that was under the reign of evil. Two fronts, two kingdoms, two economies hit head on. And in the resurrection and ascension, Christ came out the victor, Satan the loser.

It was in this, the ultimate power encounter, that salvation was secured for all men and women who place their faith in Christ. But working that salvation out is another matter. In the present age, an interim period before the coming of the fullness of the kingdom, the victory over Satan needs to be applied in the lives of people still under his power. Many Christians do not adequately recognise that though Christ's victory is irreversible, its application to everyday events is ongoing. Satan is still alive and well, even though his time on earth is limited.

Oscar Cullmann offers an analogy that helps us understand how, though defeated, Satan still has great power, power that can kill if left unchecked. During the Second World War, most military experts agree, victory for the Allies was assured on D-Day (6 June 1944), the day they successfully invaded Nazi-occupied Europe on the Normandy beaches. Because Germany failed to prevent their entrance, victory for the British, American and Canadian forces was inevitable. But it took eleven months for the Allies actually to end the war. During this time thousands of men lost their lives in the bloodiest battles of the entire conflict. The coming VE Day (8 May 1945) was assured but not realised.[1] We are in a similar position as Christians: the final and full establishment of the kingdom of God, with Christ as its head, was assured at the resurrection, but we have yet to realise its fullness in the days in which we live.

We too are soldiers, members of Christ's army. Paul instructs Timothy, 'Endure hardship with us like a good soldier of Christ Jesus' (2 Tim. 2:3). There is a war yet to be fought, an enemy still capable of inflicting great harm – if we allow him to. We must equip ourselves by allowing the power of the Spirit to come into our lives and work through us to defeat the enemy.

* * *

The unity of the early Christians was a crucial ingredient for their experiencing the power of the Spirit. In the book of Acts, when Christians are described as being together in heart and mind, the power of God comes in extraordinary measure. They were 'together in one place' (2:1), and Pentecost happened (2:2–13). They 'devoted themselves to the apostles' teaching and to the fellowship' (2:42), and 'many wonders and miraculous signs were done' (2:43). They 'were one in heart and mind' (4:32), and 'with great power the apostles continued to testify' (4:33).

In chapter 2 we described the birth of a warrior nation, the army of God, the Church. In this nation we discover God's response to people's earlier attempt to unify as 'one people speaking the same language' at the Tower of Babel (Gen. 11:1–9). Against the backdrop of the failure at Babel we learn a principle of spiritual unity from God's victory at Pentecost. At Babel, while observing the nations' attempt to make a name for themselves, the Lord said, 'If as one people speaking the same language they have begun to do this, *then nothing they plan to do will be impossible* for them. Come, let us go down and confuse their language so they will not understand each other' (vv. 6–7, emphasis mine).

God readily acknowledges that power is present when people are united in purpose and language. Even the most rebellious and selfish people, when they come together, can accomplish much of what they set out to do. The potential for good *and evil* within men and women is almost boundless when they co-operate.

At Pentecost the Holy Spirit came to produce a new nation from many nations, a new race from many races – the people of God (Acts 2:5–6, 41). Several words are used in Scripture to convey the meaning of a Christian nation. One of the most common Greek words for 'nation' is *ethnos*. Karl Ludwig Schmidt, in the *Theological Dictionary of the New Testament*, says *ethnos* means a 'multitude bound by the same manners, customs, or other distinctive features. It gives us the sense of a people.'[2] If the 'nations' of the world are always referred to as many, the 'nation' of Christ is singular, a unit. This means that, though a multitude, we are viewed by God as one people or society (see 1 Pet. 2:10; Gal. 3:6–9). This unity is one key to experiencing spiritual power.

One nation needs one language. At Pentecost God created order out of confusion, understanding of his word out of a multitude of languages. When the Holy Spirit came on the disciples, each of the others present heard them speak in his or her native tongue. Scripture describes the witnesses' initial response as being 'amazed and perplexed' (Acts 2:12). That the disciples could speak in other languages was all the more remarkable because they were uneducated.

At Babel, one nation was broken into many, one language changed to many, throwing everyone into confusion – resulting in a loss of power and purpose. At Pentecost, many nations and tongues were unified – and those present were able to experience an outpouring of power and three thousand new disciples were added (Acts 2:41).

Often in a power encounter that leads to conversion, the power of the Spirit appears first in those who are evangelising, then in those who are evangelised. People at Pentecost were 'amazed and perplexed'. Many of them, though, took a quick step and crossed over to the other side: they became participants in God's grace. Often witnessing the presence of the Spirit in a Christian will open non-Christians to the gospel of the kingdom of God (Acts 2:42).

It took Peter's explanation of the phenomena at Pentecost to lead the three thousand to Christ. Usually, when non-Christians witness the power of the Spirit, they have many questions that only the gospel can answer. A rational explanation must be added to something that transcends rationalism, the natural to the supernatural, for the most forceful advance of the kingdom of God.

An international army was born from the Pentecost power encounter. The remainder of Acts reads like war chronicles in which God's army does his bidding. Our lives should read the same way.

8

CHRISTIANS TOO

Power encounters are difficult to control and are therefore hard for many Western Christians to accept, because phenomena that do not fit our patterns of rational thought are uncomfortable: they plunge us into a world beyond rationality in which we lose control of the situation. Events that do not fit our normal categories of thinking are threatening for us, causing fear, because they are unfamiliar – especially where spiritual power is involved.

The first time I experienced a power encounter similar to the one described at Pentecost, I became extremely irritated and angry at God. It was Mother's Day 1979, and I had invited a young man to speak at the evening service of the church at which I had only recently become pastor, and which would later become the Vineyard Christian Fellowship in Anaheim, California. His background was the California 'Jesus People' movement of the late 1960s and early 1970s, and, so I heard, he was unpredictable when he spoke. I was apprehensive about him, but I sensed God wanted him to speak nevertheless. He had been used by God to lead Christians into a refreshing experience of the Holy Spirit, and it was obvious to me that the congregation needed spiritual renewal. I hasten to point out that asking this young man to speak went contrary to my normal instincts as a pastor. I take seriously the admonition that pastors are to protect their flocks, but in this instance I sensed it was what God wanted. Regardless, I was to stand by the decision, whatever the cost.

When he eagerly agreed to speak, I became even more apprehensive. What will he say? What will he do to my church? The Lord gently reminded me, 'Whose church is this?'

That evening he gave his testimony, a powerful story of God's grace. As he spoke, I relaxed. Nothing strange here, I thought. Then he did something that I had never seen done in a church gathering. He finished his talk and said, 'Well, that's my testimony. Now the Church throughout the world has been offending the Holy Spirit a long time and he is quenched. So we are going to invite him to come and minister.' We all waited. The air became thick with anticipation – and anxiety.

Then he said, 'Holy Spirit, come.' And he did!

I must remind you that we were not a 'Pentecostal' church with a broad experience or understanding of the sorts of things that began to happen. What happened could not have been learned behaviour. We had had a few experiences of healing, deliverances, and gifts like prophecy, but they happened largely in home groups or in prayer sessions behind closed doors.

This, however, was happening in our public worship meeting. People fell to the floor. Others, who did not believe in tongues, loudly spoke in them. The speaker roamed among the crowd, praying for people, some of whom immediately fell over with the Holy Spirit resting on them.

I was aghast! All I could think throughout the experience was, 'Oh, God, get me out of here.' In the aftermath, we lost church members and my staff were extremely upset. That night I could not sleep. Instead, I spent the evening reading Scripture, looking for the verse, 'Holy Spirit, come.' I never found it.

By 4:30 that morning I was more upset than I was earlier at the meeting. Then I remembered that I had read in *The Journal of John Wesley* about something like this happening. I went out to my garage and found a box of books about revivals and revivalists and began to read them. What I discovered was that our experience at the church service was not unique; people like John and Charles Wesley, George Whitefield, Charles Finney and Jonathan Edwards all had similar experiences in their ministries. By 6:00 I had found at least ten examples of similar phenomena in church history.[1]

For example, on 1 January 1739, John Wesley wrote in his journal of an event on 24 May 1738:

> Mr. Hall, Hinching, Ingham, Whitefield, Hutching and my brother Charles were present at our love feast in Fetter Lane with about 60 of our brethren. About three in the morning as we were continuing instant in prayer the power of God came mightily upon us, insomuch that many cried out for exulting joy and many fell to the ground. As soon as we were recovered a little from the awe and amazement at the presence of his Majesty, we broke out with one voice, 'We praise thee O God, we acknowledge thee to be the Lord.'[2]

I then asked God for assurance that this was from him, that this was something he – not humans or Satan – was doing. Just after praying this prayer, the phone rang. Tom Stipe, a pastor and a good friend, called. I told him what had happened the night before, and he responded that it was from God. 'That's exactly what happened in the early days of the Jesus People revival. Many people were saved.' That conversation was significant, because Tom was a credible witness. I had only heard about these things; Tom had lived through them.

Over the next few months, supernatural phenomena continued to occur, frequently uninvited and without any encouragement, spontaneously. New life came into our church. All who were touched by and who yielded to the Holy Spirit – whether they fell over, started shaking, became very quiet and still, or spoke in tongues – accepted the experience and thought it was wonderful, drawing them closer to God. More importantly, prayer, Bible reading, caring for others, and the love of God all increased.[3]

Our young people went out into the community, looking for people to evangelise and pray over. An event that I heard about is a good illustration of what often happened. One day a group of our young people approached a stranger in a parking lot. Soon they were praying over him, and he fell to the ground. By the time he got up, the stranger was converted. He is now a member of our church.

A revival began that May, and by September we had baptised over seven hundred new converts. There may have been as many as seventeen hundred new converts during a three-and-a-half month period. I was an expert on church growth, but I had never seen evangelism like that.

Power encounters in the church, in this case without regard for 'civilised propriety', catapulted us into all-out revival. What I had thought of as 'order' in the twentieth-century Church evidently was not the same as what Christians experienced in the New Testament Church.

I must add a word of caution, though. We would be mistaken to think that lack of order or organisation allows the Holy Spirit greater freedom to work, while more order inhibits him. The right *kind* of order is necessary for a church to develop to maturity and fulfil its tasks. The Church is an organism, a living body. A corpse is highly organised, but it is dead – it has no spirit within it. Many congregations are like corpses: well ordered but lacking the life of Christ. On the other hand, the one-celled amoeba, which certainly lacks organisation and complexity, has life but can accomplish little. Prayer groups and other Christian organisations that reject the need for leadership are often like amoebas: they have life but are not able to accomplish much.

What God wants is a living body, where the Holy Spirit is free to operate and the body is ordered in such a manner that it can accomplish much. This body is quite complex, because the process of evangelism and discipleship is an involved one. A key, though, is that God's order – not our own – be established. Sometimes he tips over our order so he can establish his.

9

FEARING GOD'S POWER

In Acts 5:12–16 we read of another response to power encounters: fear. 'The apostles performed many miraculous signs and wonders among the people,' this passage begins. In Jerusalem the apostles met daily at Solomon's Colonnade in the Temple, and the power of God came. At this time they were 'highly regarded by the people'. But the disciples were also feared, feared because people knew God was with them. 'No-one else dared join them,' Scripture says.

Today many churches have become so secular – even profane – that non-members have no thought or concern about entering their premises. In fact, people often see the Church as only another organisation in need of their help. I frequently receive letters from secular fund-raising organisations offering to raise money for our church. For many, the Church is an ineffective institution in need of expert advice – for a fee, of course.

In the New Testament, outsiders were afraid because they did not know what would happen to them if they moved in among Christians. They could be consumed by God's power; their secret sins could be revealed; healing could come to them; demons could be expelled. Paul, writing to the Corinthians concerning the proper ordering of the spiritual gifts, instructs them to expect power encounters:

> So if the whole church comes together and everyone speaks in tongues, and some who do not understand or

some unbelievers come in, will they not say that you are out of your mind? But if an unbeliever or someone who does not understand comes in while everybody is prophesying, he will be convinced by all that he is a sinner and will be judged by all, and the secrets of his heart will be laid bare. So he will fall down and worship God, exclaiming, 'God is really among you!' (1 Cor. 14:23–5)

God's Spirit works this way today. I recently read this anonymous account of a homosexual's conversion experience:

One weekend I went to visit some friends outside the city [in which he lived], people I knew from before my openly homosexual days. We had taken quite different directions – they were now Christians involved in the charismatic renewal – and I had never told them about my new life. However, I still enjoyed seeing them occasionally. In fact I was intrigued by their visible joy and fervor.

During this particular visit they asked me to go with them to a prayer meeting. I agreed, even though I expected an hour and a half of boredom. We drove through the steamy summer night to a large room crowded with people.

The meeting began with a few words from the leader and a couple of songs, followed by the low murmur of people praying aloud. It seemed things had barely begun when the leader was back on his feet, looking a little nervous. I can still hear him saying, 'The Lord has told me that someone here tonight has been practicing homosexuality. He wants you to know that he loves you and forgives you.'

That gentle message hit me like a thunderbolt. For years I had pushed the God of my childhood out of my mind. Now God was speaking to me. He wasn't just saying hello, either: he was asking me to give up my whole way of life.

I spent the rest of the meeting fighting with myself. 'Why do I need forgiveness?' I would think. 'I haven't done anything wrong.' Then the religion lessons of my early years would come rushing back: who God was, what it meant that he loved me, what it meant to reject him. In the end, my debate boiled down to this: 'I know enough about God to know that if he is speaking to me – and I believe he is – the only sensible thing for me to do is obey.'

When the meeting ended, I turned to my friends. 'That message was for me,' I told them. 'I want to do what God says.'

Eventually I felt ready for marriage and fell in love with the woman who is now my wife. Our life together has been my most constant source of happiness.[1]

My co-author, Kevin Springer, met the author of this testimony. Fifteen years after writing these words, he is still a strong Christian. He and his wife have three beautiful children. Reflecting on his conversion experience, he said, 'For years before my conversion I was nervous around charismatics, uneasy that God might reveal my homosexuality to them. But by the time I attended the meeting at which I was converted, I was no longer on guard. So right when I let my guard down, God's power came on me.'

*　　　*　　　*

In Acts 13:4–12 we find a power encounter similar to the one between Elijah and the prophets of Baal. Paul and Barnabas, recently sent from the church at Antioch, were in the city of Paphos on the island of Cyprus. Word of their presence had come to Sergius Paulus, the Roman proconsul, and he sent for them 'because he wanted to hear the word of God'.

The scene was set for an encounter between light and dark when Paul and Barnabas entered Sergius Paulus' chamber: present was Elymas the sorcerer, opposing them with the purpose of turning the proconsul from his emerging faith. Jesus had his witness, Paul, and Satan his, Elymas.

There was need for action if Sergius Paulus was to be fully converted. Paul, filled with the Holy Spirit, took up the challenge. He said to Elymas, 'You are a child of the devil and an enemy of everything that is right! You are full of all kinds of deceit and trickery . . . Now the hand of the Lord is against you. You are going to be blind, and for a time you will be unable to see the light of the sun.' At that moment Paul was speaking the words of God, under his unction. Elymas was immediately blinded.

And Sergius Paulus believed. Why? Because 'he was amazed at the teaching about the Lord'. What was the teaching? That the Lord was present, and was more powerful than anything in creation.

*   *   *

The Spirit can make his power felt in nature as well as through people. The result is often fear and openness in those seeing it. When Paul and Silas were thrown into the Philippian prison (they had been falsely accused of inciting a riot), God's power struck the prison, causing an earthquake, opening the doors, and loosening their chains (see Acts 16:16–40).

The jailer, who had fallen asleep, assumed the prisoners had fled. Roman guards who for any reason allowed their prisoners to escape were killed. So the jailer drew his sword to take his own life. But Paul stopped him. 'Don't harm yourself! We are all here!' (v. 28).

Paul's response to God's power was mercy, mercy extended to the jailer. Instead of fleeing for their own lives, Paul and Silas stayed in the prison. The jailer rushed to them, fell down, and asked, 'What must I do to be saved?' Paul replied, 'Believe in the Lord Jesus, and you will be saved.' The jailer and his household were saved, and the whole family was filled with joy, because they had come to believe in God. When God's power is combined with his mercy, fearful hearts melt.

*   *   *

We should not be surprised that the book of Acts is full of stories like these. At the end of Matthew's Gospel, Jesus commissions us to be sources of power encounters, ever ready to seize any opportunity to proclaim God's grace and mercy in order to make fully trained and obedient disciples (Matt. 28:18–20). I believe the great commission can be fulfilled more effectively as we open our lives to God's power in the ways that I speak of in this book.

Before commanding us to 'go and make disciples of all nations', Jesus prefaced his words with the statement: 'All authority in heaven and on earth has been given to me.' *All* authority is in Christ, so anything that he commands us to do, we have access to the power required to do it.

The Greek word used here for authority is *exousia*. Werner Foerster notes that this word 'denotes [Jesus'] divinely given power and authority to act . . . It is his own rule in free agreement with the Father.'[2] The Lord's Prayer to the Father was that 'your kingdom come, your will be done on earth as it is in heaven' (Matt. 6:10). Jesus' entire life was built on the principle of doing the will of the Father, walking in his way and doing his works. 'I tell you the truth,' he told the Jews who were persecuting him, 'the Son can do nothing by himself; he can do only what he sees his Father doing, because whatever the Father does the Son also does' (John 5:19).

All authority for making disciples is found in Christ, and he is with us today. 'Surely I am with you always, to the very end of the age,' he assures us in the great commission (Matt. 28:20).

How is he with us? 'All that belongs to the Father is mine. That is why I said the Spirit will take from what is mine and make it known to you' (John 16:15). It is the Holy Spirit who holds the key to power encounters. Our openness and availability to his direction and enabling, anointing and power is the catalyst for fulfilling the great commission.

Clearly the early Christians had an openness to the power of the Spirit, which resulted in signs and wonders and church growth. If we want to be like the early Church, we too need to be open to the Holy Spirit's power.

Study Session 2

THE POWER ENCOUNTER

Read *Power Evangelism*, Part Two, chapters 6–9.

Purpose

In this session you will examine barriers in culture that prevent you from spreading the gospel. Your goal is a heightened awareness of how spiritual warfare affects evangelism.

Discussion

Share your evangelistic experiences from the previous week. Address these questions:

- What frustrations did you experience in sharing?
- What internal struggles did you have when you attempted to approach someone?
- Did you sense God's leading – both to the person you talked with and in what you said?

Further Discussion

The leader should lead an open discussion exploring the points raised below. Many barriers in ourselves to sharing the gospel fit into the following categories. Can you identify any of them in yourself?

- *Fears* of being ridiculed and rejected; of appearing fanatical or weird; of turning people off. In fact, sometimes we *will* be rejected, appear fanatical, and turn people off. Pray for courage to overcome these fears and share the gospel appropriately and with boldness.
- *Feeling we are 'imposing' our ideas on others.* Yet these are not 'our ideas', they are the way of life to the source of life. The idea that we are 'imposing' comes from the world, to cut people off from eternal life.
- *We are not convinced in our hearts that personal evangelism is our job.* It is true that the Father draws us, the Son saves, and the Holy Spirit bears witness (John 15:26). But 1 Peter 2:9 says we are to 'declare the praises of him who called [us] out of darkness into his wonderful light', and 3:15 says we are always to be prepared to witness.
- *We do not believe that we will do any good, because we have forgotten the source of power in our witness.* With prayer and reliance on the Holy Spirit, our words become life and our action testifies that God is alive.
- *We do not know what to say.* We need to learn the basics of the gospel and how to communicate them in a natural way. But this is easy to do, as we'll learn in Part Three.

The following are what *should* motivate us this week. Have a different person look up one Scripture for each point and discuss it with the group:

- *God's nature.* Because God is love, his love should motivate us to love others and share the gospel with them (Isa. 65:2; Jer. 31:3; 2 Cor. 5:11–15).
- *Human need.* There is only one way to God, and any other way dooms men and women to hell (Luke 2:30– 2; 1 John 1:1–4). Grief for the lost is valid motivation (1 Cor. 9:16).
- *Obedience to Christ.* We have been called to evangelism (Matt. 28:18–20).
- *Eternal rewards.* Daniel 12:3 says, 'those who lead

many to righteousness [will shine] like the stars for ever and ever' (also see Mark 10:29–31).

Plan of Action

Review your list of five people from the previous week, adding or deleting any names. In the column to the right of each name, list barriers that you recognise in yourself or in them that prevent you from sharing more fully. Pray for each person daily, asking God for the opportunity to talk with one of them this week, and for the wisdom and courage to overcome barriers.

NAME	BARRIERS
1.	
2.	
3.	
4.	
5.	

For Next Week

Designate one person in the group to look ahead to next week's study session and prepare (in writing) their three-minute testimony for the rest of the group.

Come prepared to share your evangelistic experience with the group.

Read *Power Evangelism*, Part Three, chapters 10–13.

PART THREE

Power Evangelism

10

A REMARKABLE ENCOUNTER

It was the end of a long day of ministry and I was exhausted. I had just completed a teaching conference in Chicago and was flying off to another speaking engagement in New York. I was looking forward to the plane ride as a chance to relax for a few hours before plunging back into teaching. But it was not to be the quiet, uneventful trip I had hoped for.

Shortly after takeoff, I pushed back the reclining seat and adjusted the seat belt, preparing to relax. My eyes wandered around the cabin, not looking at anything in particular. Seated across the aisle from me was a middle-aged man, a businessman, to judge from his appearance, but there was nothing unusual or noteworthy about him. But in the split second that my eyes happened to be cast in his direction, I saw something that startled me.

Written across his face in very clear and distinct letters I thought I saw the word 'adultery'. I blinked, rubbed my eyes, and looked again. It was still there. 'Adultery.' I was seeing it not with my eyes, but in my mind's eye. No one else on the plane, I am sure, saw it. It was the Spirit of God communicating to me. The fact that it was a spiritual phenomenon made it no less real.

By now the man had become aware that I was looking at him ('gaping at him' might be a more accurate description).

'What do you want?' he snapped.

As he spoke, a woman's name came clearly to mind. This was more familiar to me; I had become accustomed to the

Holy Spirit bringing things to my awareness through these kinds of promptings.

Somewhat nervously, I leaned across the aisle and asked, 'Does the name Jane [not her real name] mean anything to you?'

His face turned ashen. 'We've got to talk,' he stammered.

The plane we were on was a jumbo jet, the kind with a small upstairs cocktail lounge. As I followed him up the stairs to the lounge, I sensed the Spirit speaking to me yet again. 'Tell him if he doesn't turn from his adultery, I'm going to take him.'

Terrific. All I had wanted was a nice, peaceful plane ride to New York. Now here I was, sitting in the plane's cocktail lounge with a man I had never seen before, whose name I didn't even know, about to tell him God was going to take his life if he didn't stop his affair with some woman.

We sat down in strained silence. He looked at me suspiciously for a moment, then asked, 'Who told you that name?'

'God told me,' I blurted out. I was too rattled to think of a way to ease into the topic more gracefully.

'*God* told you?' He almost shouted the question, he was so shocked by what I had said.

'Yes,' I answered, taking a deep breath. 'He also told me to tell you . . . that unless you turn from this adulterous relationship, he is going to take your life.'

I braced myself for what I was sure would be an angry, defensive reaction, but to my relief the instant I spoke to him, his defensiveness crumbled and his heart melted. In a choked, desperate voice he asked me, 'What should I do?'

At last I was back on familiar ground. I explained to him what it meant to repent and trust Christ, and invited him to pray with me. With hands folded and head bowed, I began to lead him in a quiet prayer. 'O God . . .'

That was as far as I got. The conviction of sin that had built up inside him seemed virtually to explode. Bursting into tears, he cried out, 'O *God*, I'm so sorry' and launched into the most heartrending prayer of repentance I had ever heard.

It was impossible, in such cramped quarters, to keep hidden what was happening. Before long everyone in the cocktail lounge was intimately acquainted with this man's past sinfulness and present contrition. The flight attendants were even weeping right along with him.

When he finished praying and regained his composure, we talked for a while about what had happened to him.

'The reason I was so upset when you first mentioned that name to me', he explained, 'was that my wife was sitting in the seat right next to me. I didn't want her to hear.'

I knew he wasn't going to like what I said to him next.

'You're going to have to tell her.'

'I am?' he responded weakly. 'When?'

'Better do it right now,' I said gently.

The prospect of confessing to his wife was, understandably, somewhat intimidating, but he could see there was no other way. So again I followed him, down the stairs and back to our seats.

I couldn't hear the conversation over the noise of the plane, but I could see his wife's stunned reaction, not only to his confession of infidelity, but also to his account of how the stranger sitting across the aisle had been sent by God to warn him of the consequences of his sin. Eyes wide with amazement (and probably terror!), she stared first at her husband, then at me, then back at her husband, then back at me, as the amazing story unfolded. In the end the man led his wife to accept Christ, right there on the plane.

There was little time to talk when we got off the plane in New York. They didn't own a Bible, so I gave them mine. Then we went our separate ways.

11

POWER EVANGELISM

The story in the previous chapter might seem like an unusual, if not bizarre, event, yet I could write hundreds of other accounts like it – both from my own experience and from that of others I know. I call this type of encounter *power evangelism*, and I believe it was one of the most effective means of evangelism in the early Church.[1] Further, power evangelism appears to have been present during periods of great missionary expansion and renewal throughout church history (see Appendix A).

By power evangelism I mean a presentation of the gospel that is rational but that also transcends the rational (though it is in no way 'irrational' or anti-rational). The explanation of the gospel – the clear proclamation of the finished work of Christ on the cross – comes with a demonstration of God's power through signs and wonders. Power evangelism is a spontaneous, Spirit-inspired, empowered presentation of the gospel. Power evangelism is preceded and undergirded by demonstrations of God's presence, and frequently results in groups of people being saved. Signs and wonders do not save; only Jesus and his substitutionary work on the cross saves.

Through these encounters people experience the presence and power of God. Usually this takes the form of words of knowledge (such as were given to me about the man on the plane), healing, prophecy, and deliverance from evil spirits. In power evangelism, resistance to the gospel is overcome by the demonstration of God's power, and receptivity to Christ's claims is usually very high.

Before exploring power evangelism further, however, a healthy word of clarification and caution is needed. The Bible does not teach that evangelism apart from signs and wonders is invalid, or that the addition of signs and wonders somehow changes the gospel message. *The heart and soul of evangelism is proclamation of the gospel*. Many people come to Christ after hearing a simple presentation of the gospel with little other explanation or demonstration. Paul writes, 'I am not ashamed of the gospel, *because it is the power of God* for the salvation of everyone who believes' (Rom. 1:16). The implications of Paul's words are clear: God's power for salvation is through the gospel alone, and it is experienced as we put our faith in Christ.

The content of the gospel, Paul writes elsewhere, is 'that Christ died for our sins according to the Scriptures, that he was buried, that he was raised on the third day according to the Scriptures' (1 Cor. 15:3–4), and that 'God made him [Jesus] who had no sin to be sin for us, so that in him we might become the righteousness of God' (2 Cor. 5:21). In power evangelism we do not add to the gospel, or even seek to add power to the gospel. But we do turn to the Holy Spirit in our evangelistic efforts, *consciously* co-operating with his anointing, gifting and leading. Preaching and demonstrating the gospel are not mutually exclusive activities; they work together, reinforcing each other.

Many of us are suspicious of a story in which supernatural knowledge of personal sin is used in evangelism. This demonstrates how far Christianity in Western society has drifted from experiences that occurred in New Testament times (Acts 5:1–11). Yet if power evangelism is in the Bible, why don't we see more of it today?

* * *

In fact, power evangelism is being practised in many parts of the world. A closer look at regions where Christianity is on the move shows that power evangelism is a significant factor in the majority of examples of growth. On a worldwide scale, an estimated 70 percent of all church growth is among Pentecostal, charismatic and Third Wave groups.

C. Peter Wagner was a missionary in Bolivia for sixteen years. Here is what he learned about growing churches in Latin societies:

> My background is that of a Scofield Bible dispensational evangelical. I was taught that the gifts of the Spirit were not in operation in our age; they went out with the apostolic church . . . [Even today] I see myself neither as charismatic nor as Pentecostal . . . I began looking around and trying to get a handle on church growth in Latin America. Much to my surprise I began discovering that the churches that were far outgrowing all the others were the Pentecostal churches.
>
> While I lived in Bolivia I traveled quite a bit to Chile and studied the Pentecostal movement there. The understanding I got through the Chilean Pentecostals began to open me to the validity of signs, wonders, healings, and tongues in our day and age.

His conclusion regarding the key to effective evangelism is remarkable, especially when it is kept in mind that Dr Wagner is not a 'classical' Pentecostal:

> What I'm seeing, as the picture is beginning to emerge, is that worldwide there is a remarkably close relationship between growth of the churches today and the healing ministry – particularly, but not exclusively, in new areas where the gospel has just penetrated, where the devil has had complete reign for centuries or millennia. When the gospel first penetrates a region, if we don't go in with an understanding and use of the supernatural power of the Holy Spirit, we just don't make much headway . . .
>
> [For example,] in Brazil 40 percent of the population are practicing spiritists and another 40 percent have had some direct experience with it. The way the gospel is spreading there is by a confrontation: healings, miracles, signs, and wonders.[2]

Another example of what Dr Wagner describes is the Yoido Full Gospel Church, located in Seoul, Korea. It was launched on 18 May 1958, under the direction of its charismatic pastor, Paul Yonggi Cho. John Vaughan of the Megachurch Research Center estimates its total weekly attendance for worship services at 180,000. It is unquestionably the world's largest local church.[3]

'My mind drifts back to the beginning days of the church, known even then for a constant flow of God's miracle power,' says Dr John Hurston, who has been with the Yoido Full Gospel Church since its beginning. He was responding to a question about the reason for its phenomenal growth: 'Perhaps the answer . . . is the continuation of a trend modeled by Christ: "People brought to Jesus many who had demons in them. Jesus drove out the evil spirits with a word and healed all who were sick"' (see Matt. 8:16).

Power evangelism is flourishing in non-technological countries. People living in these countries are often animists. That is, they believe there are actual spirits that hold people in bondage, and the supernatural power of the Holy Spirit is needed to break their hold. A friend of mine from Fuller Theological Seminary, Dr Charles Kraft, tells about going to Nigeria and attempting to teach the book of Romans to a small tribe. After a few months, they came to him very politely and said that they appreciated his teaching but it was not relevant to their needs. What they needed was wisdom for dealing with spirits that plagued the villagers every night, something that Kraft readily admitted he was not trained to do. Under such circumstances it is not surprising that more than half of all American foreign missionaries return home after only one tour.[4]

Power evangelism is making some in-roads in Western societies. For example, a recent census indicates church attendance may be on the increase in England, with the church growing for the first time in this century. According to Clive Calver, head of the Evangelical Alliance, much of the increase is occurring among evangelicals. They have experienced a thirteenfold growth rate over the past eight years, now numbering 1.6 million. And, like growth in other parts of the world, power evangelism is a significant factor. Calver reports that half of the evangelicals are charismatics, and as many as 80 percent of young evangelical leaders identify themselves as charismatics.[5]

Because many Western Christians feel inhibited about practising power evangelism, their effectiveness is blunted. This leaves them ineffective in dealing with people who have problems with demons, illness and serious sin. Still, power evangelism is relatively new and controversial among Christians in Western culture. How I learned about power evangelism is the topic of the next chapter.

12

HOW I DISCOVERED POWER EVANGELISM

I was converted to Christ in 1963 through the ministry of Gunner Payne, a man whose zeal for Jesus compelled him to share the gospel with anything that breathed. He went door-to-door in our town of Yorba Linda, telling virtually every resident about salvation in Jesus. Most nights of the week he taught evangelistic Bible studies, patiently answering seekers' questions into the late hours of the night. My wife Carol and I were the fruit of one of these studies.

For the first year of my Christian life I followed Gunner around, learning to do everything he did. Part of that involved telling people about Jesus. I couldn't go to the market or a hardware store without evangelising someone. By the end of the year I too was teaching evangelistic Bible studies. Between 1963 and 1970 Carol and I led hundreds of people to Christ, and by 1970 I was leading several Bible studies a week, with over five hundred people involved. I was appointed to the Yorba Linda Friends Church staff in 1970, because we had personally brought so many new Christians into the church. They were truly our sheep. I served as pastor until 1974.

The majority of people whom I led to Christ from 1963 through 1974 came under 'normal' circumstances, at least as measured by typical evangelical criteria: I preached the gospel and answered some questions, and they repented and trusted in Jesus. But occasionally I led someone to Christ in an unusual way. In some instances I received remarkable insights into their lives (for example, knowledge of a specific serious sin or deep hurt), and at other times I experienced what seemed like a supernatural force going out with my sharing and drawing people to God. When I described these experiences to colleagues, they encouraged me not to talk about them. My colleagues were uncomfortable (so was I!), and felt I would lose stature if other leaders heard about it. They had no explanation for what happened. Most of us fear the unknown.

In 1974 I left the pastorate to become founding director of the Department of Church Growth at what is now called the Charles E. Fuller Institute of Evangelism and Church Growth. During the next four years I introduced several thousand pastors to church growth principles, travelling across America and visiting dozens of denominations. During this time I got to know some Pentecostals, a part of the Church that previously I knew little about. Most of what I knew was inaccurate. The most notable groups were the Church of God (Cleveland, Tennessee), the Assemblies of God, and the International Pentecostal Holiness Church. Each group was experiencing dramatic growth. They attributed it to combining proclamation of the gospel with works of power of the Holy Spirit.

Because of my theological background, I was sceptical about their claims of healing. But I couldn't write them off, because of their undeniable growth. So I visited their bookstores and picked up literature written by or about men like John G. Lake, William Branham, F. F. Bosworth, John Alexander Dowey, and so on. Their writings may not have convinced me that they had great theological insight, but they did convince me that they were not frauds. And they awakened in me thought concerning my earlier, unexplainable evangelistic experiences. It began to dawn on me that perhaps some of my experiences were somehow related to the ministry of the Holy Spirit.

While this was going on I was getting involved at Fuller's School of World Mission, where I served as an adjunct faculty member. At Fuller I had the honour of meeting professors like Donald McGavran, Charles Kraft, Paul Hiebert, C. Peter Wagner, and the School of Theology's Russell Spittler. I was also introduced to the writings of George Eldon Ladd, specifically his work on the kingdom of God. Seminary courses and reports of signs and wonders from the Third World softened my heart considerably towards the Holy Spirit and the charismatic gifts, especially as they were related to evangelism.

Also, at Fuller I met many pastors from the Third World who reported dramatic instances of signs and wonders and church growth. At first the pastors were quiet about it, but as I probed them they opened up with remarkable stories. I realised that the power of God was working in the Third World in ways I didn't think possible today. Their experiences made my earlier unexplained evangelistic encounters pale in comparison. At this point I felt compelled to re-examine Scripture, looking more carefully at the relationship between spiritual gifts and evangelism.

When I turned to the Bible I tried to answer three questions. First, how did Jesus evangelise? Second, how did Jesus commission the disciples? Third, in the light of their commissioning, how did the disciples evangelise?

*   *   *

1. *How did Jesus evangelise?* Quoting from Isaiah 61:1–2, Jesus at the beginning of his public ministry proclaimed in the synagogue in his home town of Nazareth:

> 'The Spirit of the Lord is on me,
>   because he has anointed me
>   to preach good news to the poor.
> He has sent me to proclaim freedom for the prisoners
>   and recovery of sight for the blind,
> to release the oppressed,
>   to proclaim the year of the Lord's favour . . .

> Today this scripture is fulfilled in your hearing.' (Luke 4:18–19, 21)

As I wrote in Part One, throughout the Gospels a clear pattern of ministry unfolds, repeated wherever Jesus went. First, *proclamation*: he preached repentance and the good news of the kingdom of God. Second, *demonstration*: he cast out demons, healed the sick, raised the dead – which proved he was the presence of the kingdom, the Anointed One.

The Gospels occasionally summarise his ministry. It is particularly interesting to read what Matthew thought was most significant about Christ's ministry:

> Jesus went throughout Galilee, teaching in their syn-agogues, preaching the good news of the kingdom, and healing every disease and sickness among the people. News about him spread all over Syria, and people brought to him all who were ill with various diseases, those suffering severe pain, the demon-possessed, those having seizures, and the paralysed, and he healed them. Large crowds from Galilee, the Decapolis, Jerusalem, Judea and the region across the Jordan followed him. (Matt. 4:23–5; see also 9:35–6)

Here again we see the pattern of proclamation combined with demonstration of the kingdom of God, resulting in large crowds and many followers. In the rabbinic way of thinking, what one did was as important as what one believed. Jesus passed on to the disciples his life and *his way of life*. Most people can understand how Jesus was able to preach and demonstrate the kingdom of God. After all, he was God come in human form. God heals, casts out demons, and overcomes all forms of evil. But what about the disciples?

2. *How did Jesus commission the disciples?* For three years Jesus taught the disciples how to minister from hearts of compassion and mercy, hear the Father, grow in depend-ence on the Holy Spirit, be obedient to God's leading, and believe that God performs miracles through men and wo-men. His post-resurrection commission, as recorded in Matthew 28:18–20, reaffirms what he taught them:

'All authority in heaven and on earth has been given to me. Therefore go and make disciples of all nations, baptising them in the name of the Father and of the Son and of the Holy Spirit, and teaching them to obey everything I have commanded you. And surely I am with you always, to the very end of the age.'

Notice the three objectives:

1. Make disciples from all nations;
2. Baptise them (bring them into the Church);
3. Teach them obedience to God's word (discipleship).

Jesus commissioned them to bring people fully under his reign, into the kingdom of God. This is a 'kingdom conversion', in which people come into a new reality, a reality in which the 'supernatural' is quite natural. Thought of this way, conversion involves both a change *in the person* (being 'born again') and a change of citizenship (leaving the kingdom of Satan and entering the kingdom of God; cf. 2 Cor. 5:16–17).

The goal of making obedient disciples who are integrated into the body of Christ is a high if not impossible ideal apart from God. This is why Christ promised help to fulfil the task: 'You will receive power when the Holy Spirit comes on you; and you will be my witnesses in Jerusalem, and in all Judea and Samaria, and to the ends of the earth' (Acts 1:8).

The promise of the Holy Spirit was implicit in the great commission of Matthew 28:18–20, where, just before calling the Eleven to make disciples, Jesus said, 'All *authority* in heaven and on earth has been given to me' (Matt. 28:18b). And then, after the commissioning, he said, 'And surely I am with you always, to the very end of the age' (Matt. 28:20b). The Greek word used in this passage for authority, *exousia*, denotes power which was divinely given to Jesus. Through the indwelling Holy Spirit the disciples received the authority of Christ, which is the authority of the Father.

When Jesus commissioned them to make and baptise disciples, they understood that they were to go out and do exactly what Jesus had shown them. How else are we to interpret their subsequent behaviour? This leads me to my next point.

3. *How did the disciples respond to the great commission?* An old adage goes, 'The proof of the pudding is in the eating.' This is certainly true of the great commission, because a close inspection of the book of Acts reveals that the disciples went out and spread the good news in the same fashion as Christ: combining proclamation and demonstration of the kingdom of God. The apostles not only taught what they heard, they did what Jesus did.

At the beginning of Acts, Luke says that the purpose of his Gospel had been to write about all that Jesus did and taught (Acts 1:1). In Acts, Luke continues the story of Jesus' works and teaching, only now they are done by the disciples (Acts 1:8). Clearly he implies that the continuation of Jesus' ministry through the disciples was the continuation of Jesus' ministry on earth, the fulfilment of the great commission. Notice too that power evangelism went beyond the first generation of disciples. There were the apostles themselves. Then a second generation, Stephen, Philip, and Ananias – none of them apostles – proclaimed and demonstrated the kingdom (Acts 7; 8:26–40; 9:10–19). Barnabas, Silas, and Timothy represented a *third generation* of those who performed works of power. Finally, in every century of church history we have reliable reports of works of power.

The key to their advancing the kingdom of God was the outpouring of the Holy Spirit in Acts 2. When the Spirit came on them, the disciples received God's power. Now they were able to do works of power and to preach with power.

There are at least ten kinds of sign phenomena in the book of Acts that produced evangelistic growth in the Church. In nine instances they are specifically called 'signs and wonders'. They include healing, expelling demons, resuscitation of the dead, sounds 'like the blowing of a violent wind' from heaven, fire over the heads of people, tongues, and being transported from one place to another. Acts 2:42–7, 4:32–5 and 5:12–14 summarise the disciples' ministry in a fashion similar to Matthew 4:23–5, a passage that summarises Christ's ministry. Acts 5:12–14 says, 'The apostles performed many miraculous signs and wonders among the people . . . [And] more and more men and women believed in the Lord and were added to their number.' In the book of Acts there are fourteen instances where both apostles and non-apostles preached, performed works of power, and saw significant church growth.[1]

The combination of experiences at Fuller and in the field, combined with a rethinking of Scripture, led me to begin praying for the sick. What happened then is the topic of the next chapter.

13

A GROWING CHURCH

In 1978 God spoke to me about returning to the pastorate, something I viewed with a great deal of apprehension. But with the encouragement of my wife and Peter Wagner, I resigned my position at the Institute of Evangelism and Church Growth and returned to the pastorate, a wayward shepherd coming to serve a tiny flock.

We started with about fifty people at home meetings in which we worshipped God, studied Scripture, sang and prayed. By our second year we had grown to over two hundred members and were meeting in a high-school gymnasium. (Later we took on the name Vineyard Christian Fellowship.) In our first year we did not experience the signs and wonders described in the New Testament. The next year I began a series of sermons from the Gospel of Luke. Luke is full of the healing ministry of Jesus; I was forced to begin teaching on the subject.

Soon I was praying for the sick, not because I had seen the sick healed but because that was what Scripture teaches Christians to do. Over the course of the next ten months, week in and week out, I prayed for people – and not one person was healed. Half of the members left the church. I kept preaching and praying about healing because during this period (when I wanted to quit) God spoke clearly to me: 'Do not preach your experience. Preach my word.' Though I continued to sound foolish because of my lack of results, I did not stop preaching about God's desire to heal today. (I was not claiming that people were being healed who were in fact not healed, only that, based on the Bible, more people should be healed.)

During this time the Lord taught me several things. First, it took months for me to realise that if an experience such as healing was commonly found in Scripture yet not a part of my experience, something was wrong with how I approached it. Before, I had assumed that God didn't hear me.

I assumed that Bible study, especially as approached in evangelical seminaries, was the key to being equipped and empowered to do God's work. In fact, I was to learn that there was more to being equipped than learning the Bible. I still believe in the importance and necessity of education, but I no longer see it as the sole avenue to being equipped and empowered to do God's work.

Second, I became aware of different types of faith and of how I often did not seek faith for miracles. As an evangelical, I thought of personal Christian growth as having two components, doctrinal faith and faithfulness. Doctrinal faith comes as we grow in understanding right doctrine or correct teaching. We know that we are growing in doctrinal faith as we grow intellectually in knowledge about God, his nature, his character, how he acts, and so on. Faithfulness is character growth or the development of the fruit of the Spirit in our lives (Gal. 5:22–3). And essentially I found that to be true, but incomplete.

Through this ten-month period I became aware of another dimension of Christian growth, an exercise of faith for miracles such as healing, words of knowledge, and so on. (Perhaps this is the 'faith' described in 1 Cor. 12:9.) Key to this was learning how to know when God's unction or anointing had come for a task like healing in a particular situation.

Emphasis on doctrinal knowledge and character development is good; this other dimension of Christian growth adds much more. This was a difficult lesson for me to learn, which explains why nothing happened for many months.

At the end of this ten-month period, when I was at my lowest point, a woman was healed. Her husband had called and asked me to come and pray for her – she was very ill. The healing occurred after I prayed for her and had begun a well-rehearsed explanation to her husband about why she probably wouldn't be healed. During my explanation she got out of bed, completely whole again. This was the beginning of a trickle that soon became a steady stream.

Today we see people healed every month in Vineyard Christian Fellowship services. More are healed as we pray for them in hospitals, on the streets, and in homes. We have witnessed the blind see, the lame walk, and the deaf hear.

Most importantly for me as a pastor, the people are taking healing and other supernatural gifts on to the streets, leading to Christ many who otherwise would not be open to the message of the gospel. I estimate that 20 percent of our people regularly see someone healed through their prayers. The gifts are not confined to church services. They are tools employed in reaching the lost.

D. Martyn Lloyd-Jones, in his book, *Joy Unspeakable*, points out that in the book of Acts the relationship between the anointing of the Holy Spirit and evangelism is striking: 'Go through Acts and in every instance when we are told either that the Spirit came upon these men or that they were filled with the Spirit, you will find that it was in order to bear a witness and a testimony.'[1]

Since 1978 the Vineyard Christian Fellowships have grown to include five hundred congregations in eight countries, with over one hundred thousand members. A number of our members are new converts (mostly young people) who experienced a power encounter.

Vineyard Christian Fellowships are not the only churches that have discovered power evangelism. Others such as St Andrew's Anglican Church in Chorleywood, Herts, England; Gateway Baptist Church in Roswell, New Mexico; Crenshaw Christian Center in Los Angeles, California; and Our Lady of Perpetual Help in Boston, Massachusetts, have all experienced remarkable growth, both in numbers as well as in the maturity of their members. Each has an ongoing ministry of signs and wonders.

Power evangelism is not excluded from any culture. We have seen that it can flourish in Western societies with the same results that occurred in the first century or that are reported from Africa, South and Central America, and Asia today.

* * *

Shortly after Jesus raised from the dead a man in the city of Nain, John the Baptist sent two of his disciples to ask him, 'Are you the one who was to come, or should we expect someone else?' (Luke 7:19). Jesus did not reply by giving a set of logical proofs in the manner to which Western Christians are accustomed. Instead, he validated his ministry from the perspective of a power demonstration of the kingdom of God. Jesus demonstrated that he was the Messiah by the works he did that fulfilled the Old Testament messianic prophecies (in this sense, there is logic and rationality to his response to John's disciples): 'Go back and report to John what you have seen and heard: The blind receive sight, the lame walk, those who have leprosy are cured, the deaf hear, the dead are raised, and the good news is preached to the poor' (Luke 7:22). Jesus was telling the disciples to reassure John by what they had seen and heard – the healing of the sick, the expulsion of evil spirits, and the raising of the dead.

These were not sporadic events in Christ's ministry. A close look at Scripture reveals that Jesus spent more time healing and casting out demons than preaching. Out of 3,774 verses in the four Gospels, 484 (12 percent of the total) relate specifically to the healing of physical and mental illness and the resurrection of the dead. Except for discussion about miracles in general, the amount of attention devoted to the healing ministry of Jesus is far greater than that devoted to any other aspect of his ministry. John's disciples would have understood from Old Testament prophets like Isaiah that the presence of the Messiah – the embodiment of the kingdom of God – was demonstrated in power encounters. The early Church was effective because it understood evangelism as testifying to the fact that Christ was the fulfilment of the promise of the Messiah, with powerful demonstrations of the kingdom of God that confirmed his message.

'As the Father has sent me,' said Jesus to the disciples after his resurrection, 'I am sending you.' He then breathed the Holy Spirit on them (John 20:21–2). Earlier, after challenging Thomas to believe in him on the basis of his miracles, he had said, 'Anyone who has faith in me will do what I have been doing. He will do even greater things than these . . .' (John 14:11–12). It seems that Jesus envisaged a group of people – his disciples – who would perform not only the same, but even greater miracles than he did. The only hindrance to receiving this power is lack of faith: '*Anyone* who has faith in me . . .' It was Christ's intention that the kingdom of God be spread by others in the same way that he did it – through power evangelism.

Study Session 3

POWER EVANGELISM

Read *Power Evangelism*, Part Three, chapters 10–13.

Purpose

In this session you will learn to communicate the gospel in your own words. Your goal is to learn how to share your experience in coming to Christ in a humble, honest and natural way.

Project

Write your three-minute testimony. Whoever volunteered to write his or her three-minute testimony the week before can read it so the group has some idea of what to aim for.

An important ingredient in communicating the gospel is to share who you are and how you came to believe in Christ. Your life makes the gospel believable to non-Christians, and is the first step in witnessing. It's also easy to do!

Write your testimony on no more than one page (i.e. 250 to 300 words in length). Write in a conversational style, as though you were talking with a friend. Nobody else will read or correct it, so don't worry about your spelling or grammar. Just be yourself. Aim to tell, in no more than three minutes, how you came to Christ.

Here are some tips you should keep in mind as you write:

- Keep clearly in mind what the content of the gospel is, especially focusing on the work of Christ on the cross.
- Write in the first person, using 'I' and 'me'.
- Write in such a way that others will be able to identify with you.
- Offer enough details to arouse their interest.
- Try to use Scripture, quoting to illuminate something that happened to you. Quote it from memory.
- Don't be too wordy. Remember, three minutes is the maximum.
- Don't focus on how bad you used to be. The goal is to share the King and the kingdom of God.
- Don't present your life as a 'bed of roses'. Be honest. If they know other Christians, they know that we are not perfect.
- If you were saved as an adult, it makes the most sense to write a 'chronological' testimony. This tells what you were like before you came to Christ, how you were converted, and how your life has changed since believing in Christ.
- If you were saved as a child, the 'thematic' testimony is probably best. The thematic approach focuses on how Christ has made a difference in dealing with a problem or challenge in your life. The emphasis is on how Christ can meet our needs and give us purpose for living.

Role Playing

Break up into pairs and share your testimonies. The person listening should comment on its clarity, naturalness, and so on. Aim to share it without looking at your written words. The person you are 'witnessing' to may interrupt and ask questions.

Plan of Action

Review your list of five people from the previous week,

adding or deleting any names. In the column next to each name write the key barriers that you listed last week, then pray about how your testimony should be 'customised' to overcome those barriers. Finally, pray for each person daily, asking God for the opportunity to share your testimony with one of them this week.

NAME	BARRIERS
1.	
2.	
3.	
4.	
5.	

For Next Week

Come prepared to share your evangelistic experience with the group.

Read *Power Evangelism*, Part Four, chapters 14–17.

PART FOUR

The Divine Appointment

14

GOD'S APPOINTMENT BOOK

It had been a long day at the office, full of deadlines and meetings that leave editors eager for only one thing: getting home and relaxing with their families. As Kerry Jennings (not his real name) navigated across the freeway system towards his suburban home, he fell into prayer, a habit he had developed to redeem the hours spent in traffic jams. He interceded for his family, his co-workers and his friends. He prayed about an article he was writing. Then he began asking God to provide opportunities for personal evangelism. Suddenly strange thoughts entered his mind, as well as the accompanying peace indicating the Lord was responding to his prayers. He had acted on these kinds of thoughts before, almost always seeing God work through him.

God told Kerry to stop at a familiar restaurant, look for a certain waitress, and tell her that 'God had something for her.' Further, God said that what he had for the waitress would be revealed when Kerry talked with her. Though apprehensive, Kerry responded to the instruction, steering his car towards the restaurant.

He did so because he sensed that God had arranged a divine appointment. A *divine appointment* is an appointed time in which God reveals himself to an individual or group through spiritual gifts or other supernatural phenomena. God arranges these encounters – they are meetings he has ordained to demonstrate his kingdom (Eph. 2:10).

After being seated in the waitress's section, Kerry began

to ponder all the reasons for not delivering the message. While he was caught up in anxious thoughts, she approached. Before he could say anything, she cheerfully said, 'You have something for me, don't you?' In response (his resistance was now gone), he told her that God had sent him specifically with something, and then two insights regarding her job and a relationship (both areas of trouble for her) were supernaturally revealed to him. Asking God for courage, he told her.

She was stunned. She knew that she was encountering God, because the only way Kerry could have known the things he told her was through supernatural means. (In Scripture this is called 'a word of knowledge' or 'message of knowledge'; see 1 Cor. 12:8.) At the end of the conversation they prayed. She cried. Later Kerry learned she was the daughter of a Christian pastor, now deceased, and that she had turned away from God. Soon after the divine appointment she gave her heart to God.

Divine appointments are an integral part of power evangelism. People who would otherwise resist hearing the gospel are instantly opened to God's word. Sometimes even the most hostile individuals turn to God when a significant need is met.

*   *   *

'Always be prepared to give an answer to everyone who asks you to give the reason for the hope that you have' (1 Pet. 3:15). That is, every Christian should always be prepared to proclaim the way of salvation. Yet what I am describing in divine appointments goes beyond the simple explanation of the gospel. While proclamation is an important element of divine appointments, it would be misleading to think of them only as opportunities to explain the way of salvation.

For example, in Luke 19:1–10, we find the story of Jesus coming through the town of Jericho. His encounter with Zacchaeus, the short and unpopular tax-collector, is an excellent illustration of a divine appointment. On seeing him, Jesus said, 'Zacchaeus, come down immediately. I must stay at your house today.' Then Zacchaeus said, 'Look, Lord! Here and now I give half of my possessions to the poor, and if I have cheated anybody out of anything, I will pay back four times the amount.' What could explain Zacchaeus' remarkable response to such a simple request?

First, Jesus called him by name. There is no indication in Scripture that Jesus had any prior knowledge of Zacchaeus. Jesus was doing here what the Holy Spirit enables Christians to do through a word of knowledge, what Kerry Jennings did when he spoke to the waitress. Second, Zacchaeus was hated by the townspeople; as a tax-collector he took from the Jews on behalf of the Romans, keeping everything (which was usually a considerable sum of money) that exceeded the Roman requirements. He was a man who probably had few friends. He had a deep need for acceptance and human companionship. Jesus reached out to him and communicated through a simple request for hospitality that he loved and accepted him.

Supernatural revelation. The meeting of a deep human need. It is small wonder that Zacchaeus was saved, that all resistance to the gospel was overcome.

There are other lessons to learn from the story of Zacchaeus as well. Many times, God works miracles in quite different ways from what we expect. Zacchaeus climbed the tree in order to see Christ more clearly, but in doing so was himself more clearly seen by God. In this regard, divine appointments have an air of serendipity about them, a surprising discovery of divine favour.

*   *   *

Illustrations of supernatural encounters like this in Scripture are not exceptional. Another example, perhaps the most striking in the Bible, is the calling of Nathanael in the first chapter of John's Gospel.

Too often Western Christians evangelise with a mindset that omits the supernatural. We operate with this mindset because we are unaware of the supernatural promptings of the Holy Spirit. Have you ever experienced promptings or thoughts similar to those of Kerry Jennings, only to dismiss them as the result of a bad cup of coffee? Have you ever experienced flashes of insight when talking to someone where you knew what his or her problem or need was before that person told you, only to dismiss it later as lucky intuition? If so, perhaps from now on you should listen more attentively for God's voice, stepping out in faith when you sense his promptings.

Sometimes we miss divine appointments because we don't understand how the Holy Spirit brings most people into the kingdom, and how critical *timing* is to our part in that process. We will take a closer look at the process of conversion in the next chapter.

15

THE PROCESS OF CONVERSION

Evangelism is a complex process in which the Holy Spirit works in the hearts and minds of people. Central to the process is communication. Viggo Sogaard offers a model (developed at a 1970 seminar in Bangkok) of the various stages that people frequently go through in coming to full maturity in Christ (the letters are not labels for the successive stages; they are meant to show a progression or scale only).

S	A	Knows absolutely nothing about the gospel
O		
W	D	Had initial exposure to the gospel
I		
N	G	Understands some basic characteristics of the gospel
G		
	J	Understands implications of the gospel and way of salvation
R	M	
E		
A	N	
P		Decision
I	O	
N		
G	R	
R		New Christian
E	U	
F		Mature Christian and lay leader
I		
N	X	Mature and trained leader who is able to teach others
I		
N		
G	Z	

In commenting on his model, Sogaard says:

> It should be noted that the model indicates stages, which themselves are processes. Reaping is indicated as a process, and the model has a 'conversion point' only for the sake of illustration. The decision point could be at almost any point on the scale, but experience indicates that conversions that are genuine and lasting usually take place after a person has understood the basic characteristics of the gospel. Conversions would therefore usually take place in the area indicated as reaping.[1]

The goal of the evangelism process is to move people along the scale from A to Z, not only to a personal conversion experience but also to maturity in Christ.

But this model for understanding the conversion process is deficient. A second dimension, people's attitudes, is also significant in the process. James F. Engel in his 'Engel Scale' draws from secular research on attitudes in business and politics to show how attitudes affect the evangelism process.[2] The Engel Scale integrates knowledge, belief, attitude, intention, and decision-making to help us understand conversion. (C. Peter Wagner adds to the Engel Scale stages of discipleship training and witnessing in word and lifestyle for Christ.)

Most Christians, unaware of the Engel Scale, move non-Christians along this scale haphazardly. For example, if we talk with a person who has barely any awareness that there is a Supreme Being (−8 on the Engel Scale) in the same way as with someone who grasps the personal implications of the gospel (−5), we will speak a message he or she cannot understand. Of course, poor or no training in personal evangelism is a primary contributor to Christians incorrectly perceiving non-Christians' attitudes and thinking.

Power evangelism cuts through much resistance that comes from ignorance or negative attitudes; that is, it moves people along the Engel Scale quickly, especially overcoming negative attitudes towards Christianity. By

SPIRITUAL-DECISION PROCESS

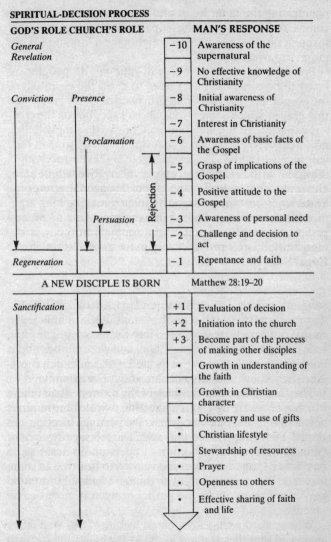

GOD'S ROLE	CHURCH'S ROLE		MAN'S RESPONSE
General Revelation		−10	Awareness of the supernatural
		−9	No effective knowledge of Christianity
Conviction	*Presence*	−8	Initial awareness of Christianity
		−7	Interest in Christianity
	Proclamation	−6	Awareness of basic facts of the Gospel
		−5	Grasp of implications of the Gospel
		−4	Positive attitude to the Gospel
	Persuasion	−3	Awareness of personal need
		−2	Challenge and decision to act
Regeneration		−1	Repentance and faith

Rejection

A NEW DISCIPLE IS BORN   Matthew 28:19–20

Sanctification		+1	Evaluation of decision
		+2	Initiation into the church
		+3	Become part of the process of making other disciples
		•	Growth in understanding of the faith
		•	Growth in Christian character
		•	Discovery and use of gifts
		•	Christian lifestyle
		•	Stewardship of resources
		•	Prayer
		•	Openness to others
		•	Effective sharing of faith and life

Adapted from, *What's Gone Wrong With The Harvest?* (Zondervan 1975.)
James F. Engel and Wilbert Norton.

penetrating the inner heart and consciousness, God overcomes resistance with the supernatural; resistance that
through rational means alone might take a lifetime – if not
more – to overcome.

Power evangelism is not anti-rational. If people are
going to be converted, they need to know the essentials of
the gospel, that they are sinners in need of God's grace, and
that grace – which comes from Christ's sacrifice on the cross
– is experienced through faith in Christ. But simply telling
non-believers about Christ does not necessarily mean they
will believe in him. Power evangelism – even receiving a
miracle – also doesn't necessarily mean they will believe.
However, demonstrating the gospel through the gifts of the
Spirit supports our message, frequently making long arguments unnecessary, so non-believers know God's love and
power. So by providing both information and power demonstration, we can effectively move people through the
Engel Scale.

*   *   *

Several years ago, when the Vineyard Christian Fellowship
was meeting in a high-school gymnasium, a middle-aged
couple out for a walk wandered into the meeting. They had
seen parked cars outside the school and were curious about
the gathering; they never suspected it was a church meeting. They knew virtually nothing about Christianity.

They found a seat in the back of the room (we had begun
worship and were singing), and within two or three minutes
began to cry. They did not even know what the meeting was
about! They simply liked the music and felt the presence of
God. For a reason they did not understand it made them
cry. When I asked anyone who wanted to be saved to come
forward, they responded, even though I had not presented
any information about the gospel or what it meant to be
saved.

When asked what they wanted by one of our staff, they
answered that they did not know – they had come forward
because they could not stop themselves. On hearing a

simple presentation of the gospel, they committed themselves to Christ.

God's timing and power overcame all reservations. Here we see the wooing power of God operating on a level that goes beyond rationality. They were drawn not by a message but by a supernatural presence. The message of the cross had to be given to complete the process, but without the leading of the Holy Spirit the couple would not have readily accepted it.

The Holy Spirit usually arranges divine appointments at critical junctures in people's lives, times when they are struggling with problems or deep needs. They may be concerned with a fear of death, a desire for happiness or success, an addiction, a character flaw, or a relationship problem. All of these are launching points to conversion, which is the topic of the next chapter.

16

LAUNCHING POINTS

Scripture contains several illustrations of divine appointments. Probably the most familiar in the life of Christ is the story of the Samaritan woman at Jacob's well (John 4:4–30). After asking her for a drink of water, Jesus used water as a launching point to explain spiritual truths. As the dialogue continued it became apparent that the woman had little accurate knowledge about the true nature of God.

Then Jesus said, 'You have had five husbands, and the man you now have is not your husband.' With this statement, he caught her attention. 'Sir, I can see that you are a prophet,' she said. That is, she realised that Christ was a seer, someone who can see the unknown – in this case her secret sins. After that she did not resist what Christ was saying. The result was that she believed. Through her testimony a revival started in the Samaritan community. 'Come, see a man who told me everything I ever did. Could this be the Christ?' Through this divine appointment the Samaritan woman moved from some knowledge of God to repentance, from sin to faith in Christ – all in a matter of minutes!

Divine appointments are not confined to the first century. I have heard testimonies of many in my church. For example, in January 1990 Luana DeWitt, a member of the Anaheim Vineyard Christian Fellowship, experienced a remarkable vision that led to the confrontation of a man's serious sin and to his conversion. Luana and her husband Chris were involved with a Christian halfway house for recently paroled prison inmates. While praying one morning for an evening Bible study group at the halfway house, Luana saw in her mind the picture of a tattoo with the word 'PRIDE'. She did not know its significance, so she gave it no more thought.

That evening at the halfway house Luana began sensing God saying that the man sitting on the floor directly in front of her had raped a woman and had not been caught. Only he and his victim knew about the rape. Luana was unsure if this was God speaking to her, but she sensed more details coming from the Holy Spirit: the woman he had raped was named 'Cheryl'; the man (she later learned his name was Ross) was ashamed of his horrible secret; and God had brought him to the meeting.

Still, Luana was not sure if she was hearing God's voice or her overworked imagination. The idea of accusing someone of rape on a 'sense' from God made her uncomfortable. She had decided to keep it to herself until he turned around and she saw a tattoo on his arm: 'PRIDE'. It was identical to the one she had seen earlier in the day during prayer. Luana felt the tattoo verified that she was hearing from God about Ross. Next she sensed the Lord saying, 'Just the opposite of pride lives in his heart. He's full of self-hatred because of shame.'

After her husband Chris finished teaching, he allowed an opportunity for people to receive prayer. Luana asked two male leaders to join her in praying for Ross. She told him what she had seen and heard from God. For a few moments he made no response, then he said, 'Ya, it's true.'

Luana said, 'The Lord's brought all of this out. He knows everything. He still can forgive you.' She then turned the ministry time over to the two men and left. A short time later Ross gave his heart and past sins to Christ.

* * *

In Acts 8:26–40 we read of another divine appointment involving one of the disciples. Philip was told by an angel to go south of Jerusalem to Gaza. He was then directed to go up to the chariot of an Ethiopian eunuch, a court official of the queen of the Ethiopians.

At the time the Ethiopian eunuch was reading Isaiah 53:7–8. On the Engel Scale, the eunuch was at the decision point (−2); he only needed knowledge about what to believe. In God's providence, Philip was sent to explain the next step to him. But for this to happen Philip had to be listening to God and obedient to his word. After the Ethiopian eunuch's baptism, Philip was supernaturally transported away. To this day the eunuch is honoured as the founder of the Ethiopian Church. The harvest was ripe, but a willing worker was needed.

* * *

Frequently God arranges divine appointments for people with significant personal problems. We should not be surprised at this. At the beginning of his ministry, at the synagogue in Nazareth, Jesus proclaimed that his mission was to 'preach good news to the poor . . . freedom for the prisoners and recovery of sight for the blind, to release the oppressed, to proclaim the year of the Lord's favour' (Luke 4:18–19).

Difficult or dire human predicaments are pathways to bring people to salvation. By being more sensitive to the needs of those around us we frequently find situations in which we too can 'proclaim the year of the Lord's favour'.

The story of Jairus' daughter (Mark 5:21–4, 35–43) is an excellent example of this. Jairus, a synagogue ruler, needed Jesus to heal his little daughter who was dying. While on the way to heal Jairus' daughter, Jesus was delayed when a woman who had been bleeding for twelve years touched him. She was healed. During this delay, news came that Jairus' daughter had died. In response to the message, Jesus told Jairus, 'Don't be afraid; just believe.' On entering the home where the daughter lay, Jesus told those who were mourning that the child was asleep.

They laughed at him, because they thought that he was ignorant of the facts. In first-century Middle Eastern society, everyone knew about life and death. The daily slaughter of animals for food or ritual observance made them familiar with death in a way that most modern people are not. Infant mortality was very high. Because of this, it was especially difficult for the mourners to see Jairus' daughter as anything but dead.

As Jews, they understood the resurrection of the dead to be a corporate event that would take place at the end of history, in the age to come. They did not expect an individual to be raised or that the resurrection was incarnate in Jesus. But the girl's death gave Christ an opportunity to demonstrate the kingdom of God, and in so doing the witnesses learned more about his true nature.

Many times we struggle with the same limitations as the Jews, the same inability to understand when God tells us to do something out of the ordinary – for example, to describe the secret sin of a stranger, as Luana DeWitt did at the halfway house. Most Christians miss out on exciting and powerful experiences in their lives either because they are not listening to God or because, due to their inattentiveness, God is silent.

After putting the sceptics out of the house, Jesus took the parents and Peter, James and John into the room with the girl. He then said, 'Little girl, I say to you, get up!' The response of those present was astonishment. Jesus instructed them not to tell anyone about what happened. While not explicitly stated in the text, we may infer that Jairus and his household put their faith in Christ that day.

*   *   *

In October 1984 I witnessed a similar conversion in London. A pastor brought his father and mother to a conference at which I was speaking. His father was suffering from diabetes and blindness. During one of the meetings God told me that someone in the audience was blind and that the cause of the blindness was diabetes. In this instance I received a mental picture of the man's eye with the word diabetes coming to mind. (Sometimes I receive pain in a part of my body that parallels the ailment in someone else God wants to heal. At other times I have a flash of intuition about someone. Over the years I have learned to recognise when these insights are from God and when they are a result of my imagination – or indigestion.)

I announced this to the gathering, along with an instruction that this person should come forward to be healed by Jesus. (It was a large crowd; I had no prior knowledge of this man.) The father was healed. He received sight! As a result, many other family members (his mother, a nephew, brother, and others) encountered God's power. After the meetings their testimony was, 'Now we know God in a way we never knew him before.'

My point is not that they became Christians (they already had faith in Christ), but that their faith took on a new meaning and depth of commitment. This illustrates how we can move people along the Engel Scale even after their conversion; in this instance it was to the point of conceptual and behavioural growth (+3).

Divine appointments usually affect whole groups of people. We will take a closer look at how they do that in the next chapter.

17

WINNING WHOLE HOUSEHOLDS

The goal of evangelism is not only the creation of individual disciples of Jesus; it also includes building bodies of people, the body of Christ. We have been created by God for fellowship. Right relationships are a part of God's plan for our lives. Because of this corporate or social dimension, we should not be surprised that God frequently brings clusters of people to his kingdom all at one time. Many times we are too focused on individuals, forgetting that when one member of a family or social grouping is affected, it can result in a whole family or town being won.

After healing the demon-possessed man in the region of the Gerasenes, Jesus told him, 'Go home to your family and tell them how much the Lord has done for you, and how he has had mercy on you' (Mark 5:19). He 'went away and began to tell in the Decapolis how much Jesus had done for him. And all the people were amazed' (5:20). A similar incident occurs with the Samaritan woman after her encounter with Jesus (John 4:28–30, 39–42).

We also read of a royal official from Capernaum whose whole household was saved through power evangelism (John 4:46–53). He came seeking Jesus, asking him to heal his son. After rebuking the official for needing to 'see miraculous signs and wonders' to believe, Jesus healed his son. What is unique about this miracle is that Jesus did not lay hands on the boy and pray over him. He simply declared the miracle done and told the official to go home. His son was healed. In response to the supernatural meeting of the official's need, 'he and all his household believed'.

In Acts 16 the Philippian jailer was saved after 'the
foundations of the prison were shaken', the prison doors
flew open, and all the prisoners' chains came loose –
including Silas' and Paul's. Then, after hearing the gospel,
he believed. At the end of the evening the jailer 'was filled
with joy because he had come to believe in God – he and his
whole family' (Acts 16:26, 34).

*   *   *

The story of Dr Luis Flores Olmedo and his family is a
remarkable illustration of how power evangelism trans-
forms families today. For years Dr Flores was professor of
pedagogy in the Department of Philosophy of the Central
University in Quito, Equador. He had written five text-
books in his field of learning theory, plus over two hundred
journal articles. His studies took him to Europe, Egypt and
the Soviet Union. He was also well known as the author of a
booklet on how to raise the ideal atheist family. In the
booklet he used his wife and four children as the model
godless family. Though he was not a member of the Com-
munist Party, he did hold the position of intellectual leader
of the campus Marxist movement. He took particular
delight in ridiculing the faith of anyone who might believe
in God – Catholic or evangelical Protestant.

In May of 1982, the Puerto Rican Pentecostal evangelist
Yeye Avila held an evangelistic campaign in Quito's bull
ring. Flores' wife and his oldest daughter, Gabriela, were
invited and decided to attend one of the meetings. Both
women were physically healed and as a result became
Christians. Gabriela also spoke in tongues. The younger
children also became Christians during the campaign –
despite their atheistic training.

Shortly after his wife and four daughters' conversions,
Dr Flores arrived home from the university to find his
family on their knees, praying for his salvation. When
Gabriela saw her father enter the room she said, 'Daddy,
I'm going to prove to you once and for all that there is a
God and that Jesus Christ is alive today. I'm going to sing

for you in a language I've never learned.' Gabriela then proceeded to sing as the Holy Spirit gave her words. She sang in Russian, then German, then Italian, then French, and finally in English. It was music that exalted the Lord. It was sung to a well-known tune, 'La Tabacundena', written by the professor some years before. Dr Flores was familiar with each language, and he knew that Gabriela did not know them. The experience left him shaken.

He did not sleep that night. The next morning he cancelled all of his classes and locked himself inside his office, where he trembled because of the presence of a Power he was unable to deal with. That evening he returned home to find his family praying for him. Gabriela again approached him, this time laying hands on him and prophesying over him with great authority. The Holy Spirit even revealed to Gabriela specific hidden sins in his life. The professor had had enough. He dropped to his knees, praying, 'Lord, I am a fool,' and offering his life to God. At that time, Dr Flores recalls, God picked him up off the floor and shook him like a doll, three times. In the process he was healed of a displaced fifth lumbar vertebra, haemorrhoids, and numerous allergies. He also spoke in tongues.

Dr Flores' conversion stuck. On 14 March 1989 he was ordained. Today he is the pastor of Centro Cristiano Vida Abundante (Abundant Life Christian Centre), where he leads a rapidly growing flock of over 1,100. The congregation has quadrupled under his leadership. Dr Flores also oversees an outreach ministry to 1,500 Quichua Indians living in remote districts of Equador.[1]

*   *   *

In divine appointments and the meeting of human needs the burden of responsibility for mediating the kingdom of God rests on Christians. The Puerto Rican evangelist Yeye Avila faithfully ministered to Dr Flores' wife and children, and because of their faith Dr Flores himself became a Christian. Through obedient and teachable individuals God is able to perform signs and wonders, thus moving people along the Engel Scale more quickly than normally happens in programmatic evangelism.

Not only individuals and families, but whole towns are converted when God's power is released on hearts and minds. This was a common occurrence in the early Church, as attested to in the book of Acts. The descent of the Holy Spirit, accompanied by the sound of blowing, violent winds and tongues of fire resting on the people, and the resultant tongues, drew large crowds to which Peter preached the gospel (Acts 2). When Peter healed the crippled beggar at the temple gate called Beautiful, the people 'came running', and Peter preached to them (Acts 3:1–26). In Acts 5:12–16 the apostles 'performed many miraculous signs and wonders among the people', and 'more and more men and women believed in the Lord'. The fact that the high priest accused the apostles of filling Jerusalem with their doctrine is evidence of the power of the miraculous to open doors for evangelism (Acts 5:28). When the Samaritans heard Philip and saw his miraculous signs, they 'paid close attention to what he said' (Acts 8:6). Many of them were delivered from evil spirits and healed, which resulted in 'great joy' (Acts 8:7–8).

The villages of Lydda and Sharon were converted when Aeneas, a paralytic who had been bedridden for eight years, was instantly healed by Peter. As was true of Jesus and the royal official from Capernaum, Peter used a simple and direct style in praying over Aeneas: 'Jesus Christ heals you. Get up and tidy up your mat' (Acts 9:34). Unlike Jesus, however, Peter did not heal on his own authority; Christ was the healer. The evangelistic task was made easy for Peter because of Aeneas' healing. Most people respond positively to acts of mercy and demonstrations of spiritual power. The raising of Dorcas from the dead produced a similar result (Acts 9:42), and many believed because of the miraculous ministry of Paul (Acts 19:11–20).

A certain attitude is required to keep divine appointments, one that permeated Jesus' and Peter's lives: How can God use me? Our part, as Jesus taught the Pharisees when they asked him about the greatest commandment, is to 'Love the Lord your God with all your heart and with all your soul and with all your mind' (Matt. 22:37). Divine appointments are occasions on which God chooses to do his works through our obedience, faith, hope and love. They are *his* works, acts to which we add nothing.

This is a difficult attitude for Western Christians to attain, because we are trained to think that only the material is real, that the supernatural is fantasy. The reasons why, and how to overcome them, are the topics of Part Five.

Study Session 4

THE DIVINE APPOINTMENT

Read *Power Evangelism*, Part Four, chapters 14–17.

Purpose

In this session you will explore how to keep divine appointments, and how to discern at what point people are on the Engel Scale.

Project

Share your recent evangelistic experiences, focusing on how you came into contact with people, and discerning at what point the people were on the Engel Scale (see chapter 15). Address these questions:

- Did you ask questions that will help you discern where they fit on the Engel Scale?
- Do you feel you shared appropriately for where they were at? Or do you sense you missed the mark?
- Do you believe that God moved them along the Engel Scale?
- Were you effective at asking 'pre-evangelism' questions like: 'What do you believe about God?' or 'Do you read the Bible?'
- Were you able to share all or part of your three-minute testimony with someone?

- As you reflect on the encounter, how could you have improved?
- Were there any appointments that you missed?

What we Learn from the Engel Scale

- Not everybody we encounter is at the same place in their knowledge of or attitude towards the gospel.
- Too much persuasion at the wrong time can actually push people up the scale, away from faith in Christ.
- In some ways, attitude is as important as information. (The thought that if people have enough information they will choose faith in Christ is false.)
- We need especially to be on the lookout for ripe fruit, people ready to convert. (Timing is everything in evangelism.)
- Much of what we have thought of as not being evangelism or as being failure is actually success, because it has moved people along the scale.

Moving People Along the Engel Scale

Once you discern where people are on the scale, you must relate to them appropriately:
  −11 No knowledge that there is a Supreme Being
  - It is probably best to pray for them and spend a minimum of time with them, unless God tells you differently and they want to spend time with you.
  −10 Awareness of the supernatural
  - There are very few people who do not believe God exists; on the other hand, many people know almost nothing about Jesus.
  - Our presence and lifestyle have a great impact on these people.
  - Slowly introduce them to Jesus.
  - Power evangelism is especially helpful for these people.

−9 No effective knowledge of Christianity
- These people see Jesus as 'a good man'.
- Avoid getting ahead of what they can understand.

−8 Initial awareness of Christianity
- Most of their knowledge is gained at church, and frequently it is bad knowledge. Churches are full of people needing a conversion experience.
- They are sometimes quite opinionated.
- We get nervous at this point because we begin to like these people and are afraid of losing their friendship or of getting too close to them.

−7 Interest in Christianity
- They are usually aware of a need in their life.
- They are willing to listen to what you have to say about Christianity.
- Through love and concern you become a bridge for the gospel; allow the cultivation of Christianity to happen by being their friend.

−6 Awareness of basic facts about the gospel
- They are now able to understand the significance of the words and works of Christ.
- They are often willing to come to a church service or evangelistic Bible study, because they see you as a credible witness.

−5 Grasp the implications of the gospel
- They are beginning to understand that the gospel will cost time, energy, money.
- This is one of the key points where people can easily be mishandled and lost.
- This is one of the easiest places to become fearful and water down the kingdom message. We must show them the cost.
- We may lose relationship with them for a short time.

−4 Positive attitude to the gospel
- They are beginning to be attracted to the gospel.
- They actually enjoy learning about doctrine, but are still not ready to receive Christ.

−3 Awareness of personal need
- These are felt-needs, usually a severe problem that they cannot resolve.
- They often move quickly to regeneration.
- Always look for these people; they are excellent candidates for conversion.
- Even at this point, people will rarely say, 'I now need to pray the sinner's prayer.'
- Do not assume the person is saved; you still have to show them how to pray to receive Christ.

−2 Challenge and decision to act
- The gospel is a heart message, not a head message. The Holy Spirit is drawing the person.
- This is where you actually close. Ask them to pray with you, or offer to pray with them. They might want to go home and pray alone.

−1 Repentance and faith
- They turn to Christ.

0 A new disciple is born
- Regeneration. Ground Zero.

+1 Evaluation of decision
- Satan tries to snatch away the fruit (1 Pet. 5:8).
- Jesus must be accepted as Saviour and Lord in order for us to resist the devil.

+2 Initiation into the church
- Getting people into a church and functioning is part of the evangelistic task.
- Baptism is the sacrament of church entrance.

Plan of Action

Review your list of five people from the previous week, and expand it to ten names. Next to each name note where you believe they are on the Engel Scale, and in the next column what you believe must happen to move them closer to conversion. Pray for them daily, asking God for the opportunity to share your testimony with one of them this week.

NAME	ENGEL SCALE	PLAN OF ACTION
1.		
2.		
3.		
4.		
5.		
6.		
7.		
8.		
9.		
10.		

For Next Week

Come prepared to share your evangelistic experience with the group, especially focusing on how you moved people along the Engel Scale.

Read *Power Evangelism*, Part Five, chapters 18–22.

PART FIVE

Signs and Wonders and Worldviews

18

IN THE EYE OF THE BEHOLDER

Shortly after the Second World War, anthropologists went to the Far East to investigate Asians' attitudes and thinking processes to see how they differed from Westerners'. They interviewed several thousand people and received surprising responses to questions based on syllogisms (in logic, a syllogism is a formal scheme of deductive reasoning). A typical question was: 'Cotton doesn't grow in cold-weather countries. England is a cold-weather country. Does cotton grow in England?' The majority of Asians who answered the question said that they were not qualified to answer because they hadn't been to England.

In Western nations, even young schoolchildren would have responded, 'No. Cotton cannot grow in England. It is too cold.' From earliest childhood, Western people are trained in deductive reasoning; we draw conclusions based on rules of logic to guide our lives. The presuppositions of our society encourage us to think this way. The assumptions of most Eastern, African and South American societies do not. Their peoples think more concretely and pictorially. The exception to this is found among those with Western schooling. (I am not implying that our society is superior to the others, only that it is different.)

The anthropologists doing research in Asia discovered that Asians have a different way of understanding how the world works. For example, they are heavily influenced by animism, the belief that material objects possess a soul or spirit. They believe that spirits determine events, and because spirits are fickle and unpredictable, deductive reasoning does not help in knowing what might occur. Asians were not comfortable predicting whether cotton would grow in England even if they were told climatic conditions were not right.

To understand why Asians interpret the world this way, we must take a closer look at how worldviews affect their – and our – thinking. James Sire defines a worldview as 'a set of presuppositions (or assumptions) which we hold (consciously or subconsciously) about the basic makeup of our world'.[1] Most of us do not consciously learn our worldview so much as 'absorb' it from our surrounding society. It is passed on from generation to generation with minimal change, the assumptions rarely being reviewed or revised. We *assume* that the way we understand life is how everybody does (or should), that *our* understanding of the world *is* reality.

Every society has presuppositions, some conscious, most unconscious. We acquire paradigms – thinking patterns by means of which we interpret our experiences – from parents, the media, art, education, and so on. Our worldview is like a lens – it colours, clarifies, classifies, warps, or partially excludes the world. It is, in Charles Kraft's words, our 'control box' of reality.[2]

*   *   *

Dr Kraft, in his book *Christianity with Power*, gives a more comprehensive definition of a worldview as

> the culturally structured assumptions, values, and commitments underlying a people's perception of REALITY. [Kraft defines REALITY, in caps, as what is actually there (as God sees it); reality, with a small 'r', is how human beings understand things.] Worldview is the major influence on how we perceive REALITY. In terms of its worldview assumptions, values, and commitments, a society structures such things as what its people are to believe, how they are to picture reality, and how

and what they are to analyze. People interpret and react on this basis reflexively without thinking.[3]

A worldview is necessary in the formation and maintenance of a society. As Christians, our goal is not to shed entirely the worldview of whatever society we might live in. Instead, our goal is to become conscious of our worldview and alter it to exclude values that are contrary to Christianity. Dr Kraft points out four functions of a worldview.

A worldview provides an *explanation* of how and why things are as they are, and how and why they continue or change. These explanations are passed on from generation to generation through folklore, myth, and stories. They give the culture a subconscious legitimacy in the minds of the people.

A worldview serves as the basis for *evaluation*, for judging and validating experience. It is a yardstick with which people measure events and circumstances in the society; it provides the criteria of acceptability.

For example, we find in the United States a worldview in which personal influence and material affluence are very important to life. This results in equating success with noticeable influence and material affluence. These worldview values affect American Christians too. They might reject conspicuous material consumption and status-seeking lifestyles, but frequently their way of judging 'successful' churches nevertheless reflects the general society's worldview: large congregations with big budgets are successful. When the Vineyard Christian Fellowship was a small, struggling – and controversial – church, I was shunned by many former colleagues and friends. Then we began to draw large numbers of people. Suddenly the Vineyard Christian Fellowship became a legitimate institution, acceptable in their eyes even though our so-called controversial teachings and practices had not changed. We had met their criteria for success: a large and growing membership and budget.

A worldview provides *psychological reinforcement* for a

society's way of life. It creates a 'we-they' dynamic: through a common worldview people identify with their society and see it as separate and distinct from all other societies. By accepting and living out the society's world-view, one feels a part of the larger group. This provides a sense of safety from fear of foreign values that might disrupt family, occupation or religion. It also creates an environment in which relationships can grow – people are fairly confident that their neighbours see the world as they do, so they freely interact. A sense of community and membership of the clan, tribe or nation is a by-product of this psychological reinforcement. As the worldview is con-tinually reinforced, the community is strengthened.

A worldview provides *integrating and adapting functions* for new information, values, philosophies and experiences. Not all new understandings that are contrary to a society's worldview are rejected outright. Some are accepted and allowed to alter the perceptions of those who accept them, eventually creating a change in worldview. In this respect, worldviews are always evolving. People who hold to out-moded worldviews and resist change isolate themselves from the rest of the world.

Many pre-modern, less technological societies, such as American Indians or African tribal peoples, have, under the pressures of European perspectives, become highly vulnerable to outside influences and fragile. Their world-views, then, have been radically altered as modern tech-nological societies moved in on them. Such an invasion has had a shattering impact, leaving serious social problems in its wake, as the history of the American Indian all too tragically illustrates.

Secularised Western worldviews have thus influenced societies that are highly penetrable but resistant to change in their overall make-up. Meanwhile, certain ideas from, or aspects of non-Western worldviews (for example, those found in Near Eastern, Oriental and even American Indian societies) have been easily accepted into some segments of Western society. After a time, however, such alien views become blunted, absorbed, digested, transformed – usually losing their vitality and ability to influence the society profoundly. This absorbing, digesting and blunting process also affects Christian ideas and values, tacitly secularising the faith. This is the topic of the next chapter.

19

THE EXCLUDED MIDDLE

Forbes magazine is perhaps an unusual source for learning about Western worldviews and the Holy Spirit. But in an October 1990 article on Brazil's economy, John Maroom, Jr., candidly observes that the Western media have largely ignored the most significant economic factor in Latin America: a Christian revival 'that centers on an evangelical Protestantism':

> When the foreign media notice Brazil, it is for President Fernando Collor de Mello's unorthodox economic policies, for Brazil's staggering external debt or for the current wave of kidnappings there. In the long run, however, what is happening in these evangelical churches has far more meaning for the future of Latin America. In these sometimes humble, sometimes grandiose churches, great historical forces are at work.[1]

Evangelicalism, Maroom claims, creates a new social atmosphere, one that is more compatible with democracy and capitalism. Individuals, encouraged to change their lives through faith in Christ, no longer resign themselves to their social and economic positions. 'The potential is quite literally revolutionary,' he writes, 'more so than Fidel Castro or Che Guevara could ever be.'[2] Maroom wonders if the spread of evangelicalism is laying the cultural foundation for significant economic and social changes in Latin American society. He concludes:

> The possibility [for transformation] cannot be dismissed.

The specific Pentecostal message focuses overwhelmingly on an individual's decision to accept Christ as personal savior. But with this message comes an emphasis on individual responsibility and sacrifice that is highly compatible with capitalism, free enterprise, a thoroughly decentralized society.[3]

Similar revivals are occurring in many countries throughout Central and South America – Guatemala, Nicaragua and Argentina being the best examples. Yet, with few exceptions, the Western media have failed to report on them. Why?

I do not believe it is because Western journalists and intellectuals are conspiring to exclude from society all reports of religion. For that they would have to acknowledge religion is a phenomenon that has a significant impact on politics and economics. Rather, unlike the *Forbes* reporter, most Westerners are *incapable* of attaching cultural significance to religious or 'spiritual' ideas and events. It is as if they have a filter that removes religion from their public consciousness. They have a blind spot that inhibits their ability to see how religion can have an impact on economics or politics.

Every worldview has blind spots, those areas of life that are simply not taken into consideration or not assumed to work. Sometimes these blind spots have disastrous consequences for the society. In animist societies such as those mentioned in the last chapter, the cause of smallpox is often assumed to be evil spirits. When modern medicine, which has largely eradicated smallpox in societies that receive smallpox vaccinations, has gone into these societies to offer a cure in the form of vaccinations, it has often been refused, resulting in untold death and misery. The people were refusing something they thought could not possibly work against the evil spirits they thought were causing the illness.

* * *

Some characteristics of Western worldviews have a damaging effect on Christians' faith. For example, secularism undermines our belief in the ability of God to intervene in the physical universe. (Secularists believe in a closed universe of material cause and effect.) Christians who accept Western secular explanations of disease – and most of us do – find it difficult if not impossible to accept either spiritual causation or spiritual healing of disease.

Dr Paul Hiebert, who was for thirteen years a professor in the Fuller Seminary School of World Mission, had this blind spot when he first went to India as a missionary. He writes:

> John's disciples ask, 'Are you the one who was to come, or should we expect someone else?' (Luke 7:20). Jesus answered not with logical proofs, but by a demonstration of power in the curing of the sick and casting out of evil spirits. So much is clear. Yet when I read the passage as a missionary in India, and sought to apply it to missions in our day, I had a strange uneasiness. As a Westerner, I was used to presenting Christ on the basis of rational arguments, not by evidences of his power in the lives of people who were sick, possessed, and destitute. In particular, *the confrontation with spirits that appeared so natural a part of Christ's ministry belonged in my mind to a separate world of the miraculous – far from ordinary everyday experience* [emphasis mine].

Dr Hiebert's 'strange uneasiness' was soon tested by a smallpox plague in the village. He continues:

> Doctors trained with Western medicine had tried to halt the smallpox but had not succeeded. The village elders finally sent for a diviner who told them that Maisamma, the Goddess of Smallpox, was angry at the village. To satisfy her and stop the plague, the villagers would have to perform a water buffalo sacrifice. The elders had to collect money to buy the water buffalo. The Christians refused to give any money. The elders got angry and forbade them to draw water from the wells and made the merchants refuse to sell them food. One of the elders of the Church in that village had come to get me at the

mission station to pray for the healing of one of the Christian girls who was sick with smallpox. As I knelt, my mind was in turmoil. I had learned to pray as a child, studied prayer in seminary, preached it as a pastor. But now I was to pray for a sick child as all the village watched to see if the Christian God could heal.

He then poses the question: 'Why my uneasiness both with reading the scripture and in the Indian village? Was the problem, at least in part, due to my own worldview – to the assumptions I as a Westerner made about the nature of reality and the way I viewed the world?' He then answers his own question:

People in the Indian villages have many diseases, curses of barrenness on women, bad tempers, bad luck, being possessed by spirits, and black magic practices. The Indian villagers have traditional ways of dealing with diseases.

1. Serious life threatening cases: With these cases they take the person to a *sadhu* – a 'saint.' This is a person of the gods who claims to heal by prayer. Because [the] god knows everything they ask no questions. Because they are spiritual they charge no fees. But one is expected to give if a cure comes about.

2. Supernatural cases: With these cases they go to a *Mantrakar* – a 'magician.' This one curses by knowledge and control of supernatural forces and spirits, believed to be here on earth. They work with chants and visual symbols to control the forces and spirits. They ask no questions, receive no fees.

3. Medicine: Some people would go to doctors who cure by means of scientific knowledge based on medicine. They ask no questions but diagnose by feeling wrists, stomachs, etc. They charge high fees and give a guarantee that one only pays if the patient is healed.

4. Quacks: These people heal with folk remedies. They ask questions, charge low fees, give no guarantees. The people being treated have to pay before receiving

treatment. (At the beginning, Western doctors were often equated with quacks.)

When [an Indian] person became a Christian, he substituted the missionary for the saint! Christ replaced Krishna or Siva as the healer of their spiritual diseases. For the illnesses they had, they went to Western doctors or village quacks. But what about the plagues that the magician cured? What about spirit possession, or curses, or witchcraft, or black magic? What was the Christian answer to these?

Because of Western assumptions, the only conclusion one had was 'They do not exist!' But to the people who really experienced these phenomena, there had to be an answer. So even the Christians turned to the magician for cures.[4]

Upon further reflection on his missionary experience, Dr Hiebert uncovered a blind spot in his worldview – and in the worldview of most Western Christians. He realised that while he believed in heaven and hell, God and eternity, he had unconsciously confined them in his thinking to an 'upper tier' of religion, far from the physical world and from his daily existence. But he lived in a 'lower tier' of science, the empirical world of our senses – those things that we see and experience in the natural, material order. The upper and lower tiers, though both were real to him, had no interaction. There was, Hiebert said, an 'excluded middle' in the way Westerners think, an inability to see how religion and science interact. The 'excluded middle' includes the influence of angels and demons on everyday life, the Holy Spirit's intervention in divine healing, signs and wonders, and spiritual gifts. Non-Western worldviews make room for all kinds of supernatural intervention in everyday life, so the idea that a Christian God can heal is easy for them to accept. But we Western Christians, by excluding this middle zone, usually make little or no room for what in Scripture is normal – the regular activity of both God and Satan in human life.

20

HOW DO WESTERNERS SEE THE WORLD?

Though some variations in worldview assumptions exist in the Western world, it is possible to speak of a dominant or majority worldview that influences us all. What key elements of this worldview have the greatest impact on Western and Westernised Christians? There are at least four characteristics that inhibit our ability to practise power evangelism.

1. *Secularism*. In his book *The Christian Mind* Harry Blamires describes the dominant element of the modern Western worldview as secularism. 'To think secularly', he writes, 'is to think within a frame of reference bounded by the limits of our life on earth: it is to keep one's calculations rooted in this-worldly criteria.'[1] The assumption of secular minds is that we live in a material universe closed off from divine intervention, in which truth is arrived at only through empirical means and rational thought.

2. *Self-reliance*. Inherent in the modern Western worldview is a desire to control everything – people, things, events, even future events. The fifteenth-century Renaissance, and then later the Reformation, created an appetite in men and women to know more about nature. In swinging away from the medieval resignation to accepting all experiences as God's will, Western society eventually swung to the other extreme during the Enlightenment, making the human the measure of all things. By the nineteenth century, materialism was entrenched in the Western world-

view, and with it came a sense of autonomy and self-reliance in which men and women felt little need for help from anything outside themselves.

3. *Materialism.* Materialism assumes that nothing exists except matter and its movement and modifications. For a materialist, only what can be seen, tested and proved is real. The scientific method is elevated to the position of Holy Writ. Working from this presupposition, Western people have learned to observe regularities and patterns in the material world and have developed a series of laws and principles for almost all areas of life: medicine, physics, philosophy, psychology, economics, and so on. These principles are thought of as consistent, stable and dependable.

A philosophy of materialism directly contradicts a Christian perspective. Materialism warps our thinking, softening convictions about the supernatural world of angels and demons, heaven and hell, Christ and Antichrist. We often live as though the material world is more real than the spiritual, as though material cause and effect explains all of what happens to us.

4. *Rationalism.* Rational*ism* seeks a rational explanation for all experience, making reason the chief guide in all matters of life. Rationalism should not be confused with rational thinking. In this book I try to write about power evangelism in a rational, reasoned fashion that can be understood by the reader. Rationalism, however, accepts reason as the only and highest authority in life. Everything that cannot be explained by human reason is rejected, especially supernatural events such as miracles. Rationalism, therefore, is a non-Christian philosophy. Because angels, demons and God cannot be scientifically measured, secularists employ rationalism to explain away the supernatural. The main reason secularists reject the supernatural is not that they believe in cause and effect, though; it is because they exclude from reality all phenomena that cannot be measured scientifically.

But twentieth-century rationalism is not necessarily an attempt to be rigorously rational. We must differentiate twentieth-century rationalism from the rationalism of the eighteenth-century Enlightenment. During the Enlightenment many rationalists thought it was possible to analyse all experience rationally and arrive at objective truth even in spiritual and moral areas. Modern men and women have given up the quest for objectivity in these areas.

*   *   *

Modern humanists – those who embrace secularism, self-reliance, materialism and rationalism – no longer believe it is possible to arrive rationally at objective moral and spiritual truth. Ironically, there are many rational inconsistencies in the way humanists think. For example, while believing in a consistent, closed material universe that may be understood only by scientific enquiry, at the same time they hold *relativistic* assumptions about religion and morality. Believing that 'whatever you believe is okay for you' assumes a plurality of moral systems. In this regard most secularists hold an internally inconsistent worldview. Lesslie Newbigin concludes that modern rationalism splits reality into 'the public world of what our culture calls facts, in distinction from the private world of beliefs, opinions, and values'.[2]

This accounts for the current growth in many Western societies of philosophies developed from aspects of Eastern and New Age thought, like EST and Transcendental Meditation. On the surface, interest in these philosophies seems to contradict what one would expect from a humanistic worldview, but most modern humanists are not rigorously rational. They frequently acknowledge there is a spiritual or moral world that lies outside the rational, which can only be known through personal experience. Even the most rationalistic, humanistic people seem to recognise intuitively that there is more to human existence than the material, the rational, the scientific. People everywhere – even Westerners conditioned to believe there is nothing beyond what scientists tell us – feel the need to reach out for something more, something beyond the rational, something spiritual. This gives rise to people getting involved in the New Age outside of Christianity, and in charismatic experiences within. This world cries for attention, but in the final analysis materialism and rationalism are incapable of satisfying it, of providing plausible explanations for meaning in life. Humanism fails to satisfy people's need to understand the universe, so they look for meaning in philosophies and religions that concern themselves with what lies outside the rational.

Christian signs and wonders are beyond rationality (not irrational), but they serve a rational purpose: to authenticate the gospel. The gospel is opposed to the pluralistic lie that says all religious experience is equally valid. Signs and wonders validate Christ's sacrifice on the cross and his lordship over every area of our lives, a relationship that can be described and understood.

21

HOW JESUS SAW THE WORLD

Many Western Christians neatly package their lives into two categories, 'natural' and 'supernatural' – with the latter quite removed from their everyday lives. Unusual or unexplainable experiences are attributed to 'chance' or 'coincidence'. The Bible, however, makes room for mystery in the relationship between the spiritual and material worlds. For example, in the Bible some illnesses are caused directly by demons, and other illnesses have physical causes. Instead of being forced to the extremes of Western empiricism or Eastern animism, the Bible allows for the *possibility though not the necessity* of supernatural intervention in all earthly experience.[1]

What, then, are some of the characteristics that set the way Christians see the world apart from how modern humanists see it? 'To think christianly', writes Harry Blamires, 'is to accept all things with the mind as related, directly or indirectly, to man's eternal destiny as the redeemed and chosen child of God.'[2] For Blamires, thinking Christianly is equated with holding a Christian worldview. In his book *The Christian Mind*, Blamires mentions several elements in a Christian mindset (the italics are mine).

1. 'A prime mark of the Christian mind is that *it cultivates the eternal perspective* . . . It is supernaturally orientated, and brings to bear upon earthly considerations the fact of Heaven and the fact of Hell.'[3] This presupposition means that Christians believe in an open universe, a world in which God freely speaks and acts. This sets Christians in

direct conflict with Western materialists, who operate on the basis that this world is all there is to life.

2. 'The Christian mind has an *acute and sensitive awareness of the power and spread of evil upon the human scene*.'[4] Evil – the world, the flesh and the devil – is constantly assaulting God's people. This awareness of evil means that Christians see themselves as members of an army, living in an alien land, locked in combat with Satan. There really is sin. There are evil spirits lurking about in the world. This awareness of evil also motivates Christians to rely on the Holy Spirit to overcome the Evil One.

3. 'The *conception of truth* proper to the Christian mind is determined by the supernatural orientation of the Christian mind . . . [T]ruth is supernaturally grounded: it is not manufactured within nature.'[5] In this regard, all experience is judged by God's revelation, whereas for the secularist truth is judged by the subjective self. For Christians, then, there are objective truths, rational understandings about God, the creation and morality, that can be known and are eternal. We believe in transcendent moral standards to which we can submit every aspect of our thinking.

Other elements that Blamires mentions are Christians' acceptance of God's authority and a high sense of the value of human persons.

At every one of these points, Christian perspectives are in conflict with the secular mind. Yet many Western Christians are unaware of the conflict, because in large part they have been secularised. How can we become more aware of those invisible elements of our worldview that have been secularised?

*   *   *

Like most difficult questions in life, the answer is found by looking at the life and ministry of Jesus. Jesus had a worldview. He looked at the world through kingdom perspectives (or paradigms) that we too can know. Charles Kraft, in his book *Christianity with Power*, outlines assumptions from Jesus' life that all Christians should hold as normative. He has granted us permission to summarise a few of these points below. (I refer you to his book for a thorough discussion of worldviews.)[6]

1. *Jesus assumed the existence of God, including assumptions concerning his nature and activities.* God is a Father with absolute authority over his children. He always loves them, though he demands obedience and faithfulness from them (Luke 15:11–32). He is actively involved in his creation (John 5:17; 15:16), stands against oppressors, and understands and relates to people on the basis of their motives rather than their surface-level behaviour (Luke 5:17–25; Matt. 23:1–36).

2. *Jesus assumed the existence of the spirit world.* This included angels, demons and Satan. The Western, secular perspective either denies the existence of the spirit world, or it fails to discern between good and evil spirits. It also fails to recognise the work of the Holy Spirit.

3. *Jesus believed in two kingdoms, the kingdom of God and the kingdom of Satan.* These kingdoms are at war with each other, and the kingdom of God is assured victory (Matt. 12:22–9; Col. 2:15; 1 John 3:8).

4. *Jesus assumed that there is a power confrontation between the two kingdoms.* Wherever he went there was confrontation with Satan, especially as he exercised his authority and power in teaching and healing (Luke 4:32, 36, 39). He sent the disciples out assuming that they too would have conflicts.

5. *Jesus and his followers received all their power from the Holy Spirit* (Luke 3:21–2; 24:45–49; Acts 1:8; 10:38). This provides a pattern for us to rely on the Holy Spirit's power as well.

6. *Whoever would lead should seek to serve* (Matt. 20:25–8). In the world, leadership is based on the leader lording it over those he leads. Not so in the kingdom.

7. *Jesus only does what he sees his Father in heaven doing* (John 5:19). This conflicts with the world's emphasis on self-reliance and autonomy.

8. *God's love is the most appropriate response both to God and humans* (Matt. 22:37–40). In the world, love is conditional and temporal, usually based on performance or emotions. God's love, in contrast, is eternal, based on forgiveness and mercy.

9. *Concern for the kingdom and faithfulness to God are the only worthwhile goals to aim for* (Matt. 6:33). These conflict with the worldly goals of self-fulfilment and pleasure, which are temporary and selfish.

These are only a sampling of Jesus' perspectives that contrast sharply with most worldviews. They affect every area of living. We are most concerned here with how his kingdom perspectives affect evangelism, especially as it relates to the release of spiritual power in power evangelism. At the very least, Jesus saw miracles, signs and wonders as *normal* events, not, as we are so often taught, as unusual intrusions by God in a world from which he is ordinarily removed.

So, what kind of worldview should we have? One that is rooted in Jesus' way of looking at the world: Power wrapped in love. We will take a closer look at that in the next chapter.

22

POWER WRAPPED IN LOVE

We have seen that a worldview exerts a powerful influence on the minds of people, and that few are conscious of just how strong and controlling an influence it is. But human beings are not robots incapable of changing their programming. A group's worldview does not completely determine the perceptions of its individual members or subgroupings at all times. We interact with contrary worldviews as there is opportunity – through travel, reading, new relationships, and contact with the worldviews of other subgroupings within our society or other societies.

Many evangelicals sincerely think that their thinking on such issues as healing or power evangelism is formed by the Bible alone. They are unaware of how powerful the influences of a Western materialistic worldview are, and how that worldview affects their interpretation of Scripture in general, and specifically their perception of the supernatural in Scripture.

Most Western Christians must undergo a shift in perception to become involved in a signs and wonders ministry, a shift towards a worldview that makes room for God's miraculous intervention. It is not that we allow God's intervention: he does not need our permission. The shift is that we begin to *see* his miraculous works and *allow* them to affect our lives.

Our ability to see and understand different phenomena is learned. Sometimes, because we have a different view of something or because we have not learned what to look for, we cannot see what is obvious to others. An analogy can be drawn from viewing the following drawing:

Do you see a young woman or an old hag? Some see a young woman, then, looking at the picture differently, an old hag. Others see only one or the other until someone shows them how to see the image differently. The lines of the drawing do not shift; the perception of the observer does. This, on a small scale, is analogous to a worldview change, a shift in perception.

It is difficult to recognise something you have not seen before. When you first see it, you do not comprehend it. Seeing, in this respect, is a learning process that takes place over a period of time.

So we do not see or notice everything we look at; we have selective perception. In the New Testament, dreams and visions are one of the means of communication that God uses in speaking to his people. They are even described as a normal part of the Christian life. Peter, quoting from Joel's prophecy, promised that the day had arrived when 'your young men will see visions, your old men will dream dreams' (Acts 2:17). Yet how often do Western evangelicals today report dreams and visions? Is it because God is not revealing himself in this fashion, or because a blind spot in our worldview prevents us from seeing what God is doing?

* * *

I went through a process of learning to see the kingdom of God, of adjusting my worldview, as I began a signs and wonders ministry. Jesus taught the disciples about spiritual eyesight in response to their questions concerning the parable of the sower and the seeds in Matthew 13:11–16:

> 'The knowledge of the secrets of the kingdom of heaven has been given to you, but not to them . . . This is why I speak to them in parables:
>
>> "Though seeing, they do not see;
>> though hearing, they do not hear or understand."
>
> In them is fulfilled the prophecy of Isaiah:
>
>> "You will be ever hearing but never understanding;
>> you will be ever seeing but never perceiving.
>> For this people's heart has become calloused;
>> they hardly hear with their ears,
>> and they have closed their eyes.
>> Otherwise they might see with their eyes,
>> hear with their ears,
>> understand with their hearts,
>> and turn, and I would heal them."
>
> But blessed are your eyes because they see, and your ears because they hear.'

This passage contains two principles about learning to see the kingdom of God. First, we need Christ's grace, his choosing to reveal to us the secrets of the kingdom. We can only see what God reveals to us. Because we live under the new covenant, the covenant of the Holy Spirit, we have confidence that God 'will pour out [his] Spirit on all people' (Acts 2:17).

This leads to the second principle, which is how we receive kingdom grace. People with soft and teachable hearts openly receive and obey the words of the kingdom. The root problem for people not receiving the secrets of the kingdom is in the heart, in our motives and attitudes towards the things of God. But the passage goes on to say that there is a direct relationship between peoples' hearts and their worldviews. A 'hard heart', closed to the supernatural, cannot see or hear the secrets of the kingdom.

There are two ways that a hard heart affects our worldview. A hard heart may incline us towards a worldview that excludes the supernatural or it may prevent us from altering a faulty worldview to include the supernatural. In either case, the key to seeing the kingdom of God and doing the works of Christ is opening our hearts more fully to his Spirit. 'But the one who received the seed that fell on good soil [an open heart] is the man who hears the word and understands it. He produces a crop, yielding a hundred, sixty or thirty times what was sown' (Matt. 13:23).

*   *   *

We see according to our expectations. Many times our expectations come from conditioning: we are taught to expect certain things in the Christian life and we miss what God is doing if he acts outside of our expectations. In Scripture, the story of the feeding of the multitude illustrates how prior conditioning blinds us to learning about the kingdom of God. After Jesus fed thousands, the people said, 'Surely this is the Prophet who is to come into the world.' Jesus withdrew from there because 'they intended to come and make him king by force' (John 6:14–15). Because the Jews assumed that the Messiah was coming in part to re-establish a political kingdom like David's, whenever they saw Jesus perform a miracle and identified him as the Messiah, they thought he had come to establish his political kingdom. Even the disciples, after the resurrection, worked under this assumption (see Acts 1:6). They had the *expectation* of an earthly king.

Years ago I was embarrassed by people in my church who talked about strange, supernatural experiences. Once a woman came to me and described her conversion experience. (She had tried to talk with another pastor about it, but he refused to listen.) She did not fully understand what happened to her, and needed help from a pastoral leader. One evening she came home from a party and on entering her house sensed the presence of someone. It frightened her, but she could not find anyone. Later, in her bedroom, she heard a voice. All it said was, 'Rosa Lee.' Her friends knew her only as Lee, even though her full name was Rosa Lee. She turned and saw no one. Then she heard the voice again. This time she asked, 'Who is it? Lord?' 'Yes, Rosa Lee. It is time for you to know me.' She fell on her face and received Christ as her Saviour.

When she told me her story, I thought she was very strange, if not slightly demented. Hearing voices? I took her through the biblical steps to salvation to ensure that she was *really* saved. She left our meeting hurt. My worldview, my expectations about how God speaks to people today, controlled how I interpreted her experience, and as a result I cheapened her conversion experience. (I thank God that years later, after growing in my understanding of the supernatural, I met her again and apologised for what I had done. She graciously forgave me.)

*   *   *

All I have said about worldviews points towards one conclusion: Christians' worldviews affect their theology. If Christians have a worldview that is governed by Western materialism, they will probably deny that signs and wonders are for today. Though they may use a theological rationale, the real issue is that it upsets their worldview. In contrast to this, if a second group of Christians have a worldview that is governed by Western rationalism, they might acknowledge signs and wonders for the thrill of the experience, as an end in itself. They do not understand one of the primary purposes of signs and wonders: to *demonstrate* the kingdom of God.

If we believe in a theology that does not include the possibility of contemporary Christians doing the works of Jesus – including signs and wonders – we will not have a practice of signs and wonders. Kevin Springer knows of a man whose wife was healed after her doctors told him she would not live through the night. The evening the doctors informed him that his wife was terminally ill, he called his church elders and asked them to come and pray for her. The elders were not convinced that God heals today, but nevertheless came out of obligation. They prayed over her, anointing her with oil, and – to their surprise – the next day she walked out of the hospital. The doctors called it 'a miracle'. What is remarkable about this incident is that the elders never told the congregation what happened! They were not as elated as the doctors. Further, this miraculous event did not stimulate the practice of prayer for the sick in the church. Why? Because their theology acted as a control that screened out the possibility of seeing it as an obvious miracle. They simply did not have a theology for the practice of healing. Even if they openly acknowledged the healing, they would not know how to incorporate the healing ministry in the church. So God healed *in spite of* them. His mercy was greater than the elders' unbelief.

In the last chapter of Acts, we read that Paul was bitten by a viper on the island of Malta (Acts 28:1–6). The people from Malta responded first by thinking that Paul was a murderer who had escaped drowning in the sea but whom 'Justice' had not allowed to live. The Maltese had a cosmic worldview: they assumed interaction between the cosmic and empirical worlds. First they interpreted the viper's bite as God's judgement. Then, seeing Paul alive, they assumed that Paul was a god. For them, only a god would not die from such a bite. The idea that God intervenes directly in the affairs of men and women was an unconscious presupposition.

Secularised people might have said, 'It must have been an old snake' or 'It bit someone earlier in the day and was low on poison.' Western Christians often think the same way, perhaps adding, 'God planned that an old snake would be there in order to save Paul.' Our assumptions about God control our conclusions as much as the Maltese islanders' assumptions controlled theirs.[1]

*   *   *

So, what are some of the key assumptions that we must hold about God and his present activity if we are going to practise power evangelism? A good place to start is by taking a closer look at the list of Jesus' assumptions at the end of the last chapter (pp. 145–6). Do you hold the same attitudes as Jesus? Do you believe that God loves human beings? Do you assume the existence of the spirit world? Do you believe there is a conflict between two kingdoms currently being waged around you, and that you have been drafted into the fight? Do you believe you can receive power from the Holy Spirit? Do you believe God can heal through you, and that he speaks to you as you listen to his voice?

A new view of God's power and action will naturally lead to a new view of his love and power. Jesus is the God of love, and he is the God of power. But what is the relationship between his love and power? Charles H. Kraft says:

> I began to ask myself about the place of power in Jesus' ministry. Was it peripheral to his real purpose, as some would lead us to believe? [Or] . . . was Jesus' use of spiritual power integral to his message of love? I came to the conclusion that *in Jesus love and power are inseparable. Put simply, that's what a loving God who is powerful is all about – especially when he is in battle with the enemy of our souls.*[2]

Jesus always used power in a loving way, never as an end

in itself. God's power always demonstrated his love. This means spiritual power for the Christian always demonstrates God's love. Power evangelism is a way of advancing the love of God in the proclamation and demonstration of the gospel.

Jesus exercised spiritual power to minister to human beings. Power evangelism was 'normal' for him, because he saw no dichotomy between power and love. In Part Six we will explore in greater detail the relationship between Jesus' signs and wonders and evangelism.

Study Session 5

WORLDVIEWS

Read *Power Evangelism*, Part Five, chapters 18–22.

Purpose

In this session you will look at how different elements of your worldview affect whom you talk with and how you talk with them.

Project

Lesslie Newbigin, in his book *Foolishness to the Greeks*, argues that a dichotomy between our private and public worlds is fundamental to Western culture, and that to be effective in personal evangelism we must understand this dichotomy. When we attempt to speak about private issues in the public arena, we violate one of society's unwritten laws. The following chart summarises public and private values:

PUBLIC	PRIVATE
Science	God
Politics	Morality
Facts	Opinions
Relative values	Absolute right and wrong
Religious pluralism	Religious beliefs
Scientific experiment	Religious experience

Matter	Spirit
Modern psychology	Angels and demons
Earth	Heaven and hell
Temporal	Eternal
Modern medicine	Divine healing
Material	Immaterial
Visible	Invisible

When talking about private matters in the public sphere, especially when talking about God, we run the risk of censure and rejection. In some instances, such as in academic or professional settings, we can lose our jobs. So it is important that we understand the context of our witness: the more 'public' the situation, the greater the chance of rejection.

For Discussion

Referring to your recent evangelistic experiences, have you felt tension when trying to bring an issue from the private domain (see above chart) into the public sphere? Has the tension inhibited you from saying and doing all that you felt God wanted you to say and do?

The following contexts have strengths and weaknesses for sharing the gospel:

1. *Close family members*. Easy access; acceptable to talk about God; more to lose in relationship (risk rejection); best long-term results; usually difficult to talk.
2. *More distant relatives*. Less access; not always acceptable to talk about God; more to lose in relationship (risk rejection); good long-term results; easy to talk.
3. *Close friends*. Easy access; not always acceptable to talk about God; much to lose in relationship (risk rejection); good long-term results; difficult to talk.
4. *Acquaintances*. Less access; not acceptable to talk about God; not much to lose in relationship; moderate long-term results; somewhat difficult to talk.

5. *Co-workers*. Good access; absolutely not acceptable to talk about God; much to lose in relationship (even your job!); good long-term results; very difficult to talk.
6. *Strangers*. Poor access; not acceptable to talk about God; nothing to lose in relationship; poor long-term results; easy to talk.

Further Discussion

Study the six categories above and, referring to your recent experiences, discuss how different contexts affect what and how we share. How important is it that we are aware of the context we are sharing in? How important is it that we challenge some of our society's prohibitions against talking about God in public?

Plan of Action

Review your list of ten people from the previous week. Go back to your chart and ask yourself which areas from Newbigin's 'private' domain (for example, heaven and hell or divine healing) each person might be open to talking about. Now pray for them daily, asking God for the opportunity to talk about the 'private' hot issue, which might even open the opportunity to share your testimony.

For Next Week

Come prepared to share your evangelistic experiences with the group, with special concern for how worldviews (your own and those of the people you shared with) affected your witness. Try and share with someone from a context that in the past you have shied away from (for example, with a close friend or a complete stranger).

Read *Power Evangelism*, Part Six, chapters 23–7. If possible, get a copy of *Power Healing* (Hodder & Stoughton, 1986) and read chapters 4–7.

NAME	ENGEL SCALE	HOT ISSUES	PLAN OF ACTION
1.			
2.			
3.			
4.			
5.			
6.			
7.			
8.			
9.			
10.			

PART SIX

The Works of Jesus

23

GLIMPSES OF GOD'S LOVE

So far I have established three premises that are the basis for power evangelism. First, two kingdoms, the kingdom of God and the kingdom of Satan, are in conflict, and Christians have been drafted into Christ's army to do battle against Satan. Second, evangelism is meant to go forward in the power of the Holy Spirit. And third, our worldviews affect how we understand Scripture, including passages about signs and wonders.

Keeping these in mind, let us now examine in more detail what Christ did, especially his works of signs and wonders. Jesus' signs and wonders were his calling card, proofs that the kingdom of God had come. Herman Ridderbos writes, 'This factual relation between the coming of the kingdom and Jesus' miracles is brought out not only by the casting out of devils but also by Jesus' other miracles, for they all prove that Satan's power has been broken and that, therefore, the kingdom has come.'[1] Jesus' miracles have another purpose: to show us what the kingdom of God is like, to reveal glimpses of God's love, peace and joy.

*   *   *

C. Peter Wagner, in *Church Growth and the Whole Gospel*, outlines two categories of signs of the kingdom found in Scripture:

> Category A: Social signs, those applied to people in general:

Preaching the good news to the poor
Proclaiming release to the captive
Liberating the oppressed
Instituting the Year of Jubilee.
Category B: Personal signs, signs applied to specific
individuals:
Restoring sight to the blind
Casting out demons and evil spirits
Healing sick people
Making the lame walk
Cleansing lepers
Restoring hearing to the deaf
Taking up poisonous serpents
Raising the dead
Speaking in tongues
Calming storms
Feeding thousands
Drinking deadly poison with no ill effect.[2]

Describing Category B, Wagner says:

> It is what the Bible refers to when it records the prayers
> of the believers in Jerusalem, 'Stretch out your hand to
> heal and perform miraculous signs and wonders through
> the name of your holy servant Jesus' (Acts 4:30) . . . The
> main function of Category B signs is to draw attention to
> the power of God in order to open unsaved people's
> hearts to the message of the gospel.[3]

Miracles are a foreshadowing and promise of coming
universal redemption and the fullness of the kingdom.
Casting out demons signals God's invasion of the realm of
Satan, and Satan's final destruction (Matt. 12:29; Mark
3:27; Luke 11:21–2; John 12:31; Rev. 20:1–3). Healing the
sick bears witness to the end of all suffering (Rev. 21:4).
Miraculous provisions of food tell us about the end of all
human need (Rev. 7:16–17). Stilling storms points forward
to the complete victory over the powers using nature to

threaten the earth. Raising the dead announces that death will be for ever done away with (1 Cor. 15:26; Rev. 21:4).[4]

*   *   *

Before taking a closer look at how personal signs enhance evangelism, I want to point out the significant relationship between them and social signs like care for the poor and liberating the oppressed. Social justice is at the very heart of the gospel. Jesus stated his mission in Luke 4:18–19: 'to preach good news to the poor, . . . to proclaim freedom for the prisoners and recovery of sight for the blind, to release the oppressed, to proclaim the year of the Lord's favour'. In the Old Testament the 'year of the Lord's favour' was the Year of Jubilee, in which debts were to be cancelled, slaves freed, land redistributed (Lev. 25). Jesus announced the impending establishment of an eternal Jubilee.

This was fulfilled in the kingdom that Jesus brought. It is a kingdom in which 'justice roll[s] on like a river, [and] righteousness like a never-failing stream' (Amos 5:24), a kingdom that 'upholds the cause of the oppressed and gives food to the hungry' and 'sets prisoners free' (Ps. 146:7).

Jesus saw the people he preached to and healed as 'harassed and helpless' victims of injustice who were powerless to help themselves (Matt. 9:35–6). He linked his healing ministry with ministry to the poor, because he saw both as 'bringing justice' (Matt. 11:5; 12:15–21). In the Sermon on the Mount he pronounced blessing on those who hungered and thirsted for justice (Matt. 5:6). He also gave his disciples a clear mandate to act for social justice: 'I tell you that unless your righteousness surpasses that of the Pharisees and the teachers of the law, you will certainly not enter the kingdom of heaven' (Matt. 5:20). Obedience to God requires private righteousness and standing for righteousness in the world (Matt. 25:31–46).

As we stand for social justice we testify to the presence of the kingdom, and our evangelistic efforts are empowered. Peter Wagner's categories of 'social signs' and 'personal signs' do not stand in opposition to one another. In fact, as we go forth preaching the gospel and standing for social justice, the Holy Spirit breaks through in signs and wonders.

*   *   *

This is what happened to Fr Rick Thomas in 1981 when he and a group called the Lord's Food Bank carried food over the El Paso, Texas, border into a jail in Ciudad Juarez, Mexico. Based on previous trips to the jail, they brought enough food for seventy-five or so men – four pans of bread pudding (each pan containing about twenty to twenty-five servings), six hundred tortillas, a large open pot of lemonade, and some lentils and chilli. But much to their surprise there were more than seventy-five men in the Juarez jail that day.

As the inmates streamed from the first cell, it seemed that the line would never end. They came and they came.

'Because we had no spoon,' Fr Thomas says, 'they were dipping the bread pudding out with paper plates. They were piling their plates high with bread pudding.'

The first pan of pudding was only half empty when the first cell had been fed. According to the jail officials, there were 170 men in that first cell.

They had to start dipping out of the second pan of bread pudding about halfway through the line from the second cell. But the pudding in the four pans lasted for all the prisoners, a total of around 250 men. And the six hundred tortillas, which were served four to each prisoner, fed the whole group as well.

'It was one of the only instances I know of where many in the community were aware that God was multiplying food at the time it was happening,' Fr Thomas says. 'You've never seen people praise God like they did that day. The people from the Food Bank were beside themselves with joy, knowing what was happening. They were dancing and praising God with great joy.

'Toward the end, some of the musicians quit playing and started carrying food for second and third helpings for all the prisoners who wanted more. They even fed the administrators and the guards.

'The prisoners were so moved,' Fr Thomas says. 'God moved on them in a great way that day. They were used to nothing but mistreatment. They were overwhelmed by the kingdom of God before them.

'I felt the Lord doing something there that day in all the prisons of the world, breaking the power of Satan in jails all over the world.'

Fr Thomas and the members of the Lord's Food Bank hadn't planned on multiplying food when they went to the Ciudad Juarez jail. They were simply obeying God's command to comfort and feed and share the gospel with the men in jail. And, in their obedience and faith, God sovereignly performed a powerful miracle.[5]

*　　*　　*

In the remaining chapters of Part Six I will explore how Jesus demonstrated the kingdom of God through signs and wonders. We dare not forget, however, that signs and wonders are expressions of God's compassion and mercy. They flow from his concern for the poor, downtrodden and oppressed. Signs and wonders, therefore, go hand in hand with social justice.

Jesus performed signs and wonders that demonstrated his love and his reign over four areas through which Satan particularly works – demons, disease, destructive nature, and death. We'll take a closer look at each of these in the following chapters.

24

POWER OVER DEMONS

In June 1982, at a meeting of the Consultation on the Relationship Between Evangelism and Social Responsibility (sponsored by the World Evangelical Fellowship and the Lausanne Committee on World Evangelisation), fifty evangelical leaders from twenty-seven different countries gathered in Grand Rapids, Michigan, to discuss social signs of the gospel. In their final report, they said:

> We believe that signs should validate our evangelism . . . The third sign of the kingdom was exorcism. We refuse to demythologize the teaching of Jesus and his apostles about demons. Although the 'principalities and powers' [see Ephesians 6:12] may have a reference to demonic ideologies and structures, we believe that these certainly are evil personal intelligences under the command of the Devil. Demon possession is a real and terrible condition. Deliverance is possible only in a power encounter in which the name of Jesus is invoked and prevails.[1]

Jesus never met a demon that he liked, and he met them frequently. Demon-expulsion is a direct attack by Jesus on Satan, a primary goal of Jesus' mission. 'The reason the Son of God appeared', John writes in his first letter, 'was to destroy the devil's work' (1 John 3:8). James Dunn writes, 'The binding of Satan was expected by the Jews as a mark of the close of the age.'[2] In this regard Christ's worldview was similar to the Jews'. Jesus came to fulfil that expectation by destroying the works of the devil and his minions.

Satan's methods of attack vary: people are tempted or inflicted with physical and emotional hurt, their lives are threatened or they are possessed by demons. Demons exert various degrees of influence over people. In some cases, such as in demonic possession, they gain a high degree of control over the human will. In Scripture, demons cause dumbness (Matt. 9:32–3), physical blindness (Matt. 12:22–3), and epilepsy (Matt. 17:14–21). Mental insanity is suggested in Mark 5, where the healed Gerasene demoniac is described as clothed and in his right mind, suggesting that before he was not. Of course, not *all* (or even most) physical, emotional and psychological problems are caused by Satan; however, in some instances they may be caused by him.

Jesus withstood Satan's attacks in the wilderness, then immediately taught that the rule of God was near (Mark 1:15). Soon after his wilderness temptation, during his first sermon (in the synagogue at Capernaum), Jesus cast out a demon from a man (Mark 1:21–8). Before being cast out, the demon enquired, 'Have you come to destroy us?' This question reveals a knowledge of what God has in store for demons at the end of the age. Jesus, through his actions, demonstrated that he had come to destroy them, though that destruction will not be accomplished fully until the age to come.

Jesus told the demon to 'be quiet' and 'come out of him [the man]'. The former phrase is frequently translated, 'He rebuked him.' It means to denounce or censure in order to end an action. What he said was, 'Stop it! That's enough!' 'Be quiet' conveys the idea of strangling or muting. He throttled the demon, and the demon left. Jesus saw the man as a victim of an unseen force, and he dealt ruthlessly with the spirit.

The disciples also expelled demons. We also advance the kingdom of God in the same way: overthrowing every contrary spirit in the name of our King. Too many Christians do not know how to deal with demons. They are afraid of evil spirits. They do not understand the scriptural basis for our authority and power over them. We can and ought to treat evil spirits ruthlessly – binding, rebuking and casting them out whenever we encounter them. (Jude 9 does not mean that Christians cannot rebuke or cast out demons, for they did so frequently, as Jesus commanded them to. The context deals with rebellious persons who 'reject authority' and 'slander celestial beings' on their own authority (Jude 8). Jude says that not even the archangel Michael presumed to do that, but depended on the Lord's authority, not his own.)

Authority over demons is power that Christ freely gives Christians. When the Seventy-two returned from their missions, they said, 'Lord, even the demons submit to us in your name.' Christ responded, 'I saw Satan fall like light-ning from heaven. I have given you authority to trample on snakes and scorpions and to overcome all the power of the enemy; nothing will harm you' (Luke 10:17–19). There is no doubt that we possess all the authority we need to overcome demons (Mark 16:17–18; Acts 1:8; Rev. 12:11). Jesus gave his disciples 'power and authority to drive out *all* demons' (Luke 9:1; see also Eph. 6:10–18; Jas. 4:7; 1 Pet. 5:9; 1 John 4:4). Jesus was acknowledging the battle that we have been thrown into on earth, that God had thrown Satan out of heaven, and that we need not fear his power to hurt.

*   *   *

In 1981 I spoke at a conference in the Anglican parish church of St Michael-le-Belfrey, York, England. During one of the meetings I was introduced to a woman in her early twenties who had been acting strangely in the back of the church. She was cowering like a frightened animal. (Later I learned that she suffered from serious metabolic disorders and an assortment of psychological problems, complicated by prolonged drug abuse. She was in constant physical and emotional pain.)

I bent over to look into her face. Her eyes were entirely rolled back, so I could see only the white parts and none of the pupils. There was a sensitivity and an uneasiness in my own spirit that indicated this was probably more than an emotional problem. (I find this sensation difficult to describe because it is spiritual, not physical, in nature.) She spoke to me in a very gruff, masculine voice, blaspheming the Lord and me. The voice told me that Jesus Christ had no authority or power, and neither did I. The voice further said, 'This woman is mine. You can't have her. Stay away.' Based on these responses, I assumed she was a demonised person.

I spoke to the demon who was temporarily in control of the woman's conscious mind, and said, 'I command you to release this girl.' Immediately her eyes rolled back down, and her voice and personality changed to that of a young woman.

She began weeping and said, 'I'm frightened.'

I responded, 'I know. Do you want help?'

She said, 'They say they will kill me if I ask for help.'

I told her that they could not kill her at that point. 'If you want help, there is help here.'

'I do want help.'

I told her to come with me, and immediately the demon tried to take over her personality again, attempting to force her withdrawal. I again commanded the demon to be silent.

We went through the crowd until we found the pastor, David Watson. I explained the situation to David, asking his permission to minister to her. He approved and asked if he too could pray for her. I agreed.

I took the girl, David Watson, and ten or twelve ministry team members into a small room in the church. Then I asked the manifesting demon its name and what it did to the girl. It told me its name and said it made her want drugs. We cast that demon out by name.

For seven hours the woman intermittently told her story and we prayed over her, taking authority over different types of demons as they identified themselves. Eventually we cast out some forty demons. During the interviews we learned that she had been in and out of state hospitals all of her life, had been molested since the age of six, and had serious involvement with the occult.

After this process she was able to repent of her sin and receive Christ as Lord and Saviour. Her life was immediately changed. (A detailed report of this incident was written by David Watson and submitted to his bishop.)

In 1982 she came to Yorba Linda for three months and stayed in the home of one of our church members. She was no longer demonised, but she still had some social and emotional problems. She received counselling help in Yorba Linda and England and overcame most of these problems. In October 1985 I was in Sheffield, England, and spent time with her. She had just graduated from the university and was beginning her student teaching. She brought with her a young man with serious demonic problems. A ministry team from the Vineyard ministered to him!

*   *   *

Power encounters with demons produce remarkable evangelistic fruit on the mission field. In 1987 John Weed, a missionary to Muslims in West Africa, came face to face with a demon. He and his wife Ruthie had been working for about a year under the Presbyterian Church in America's missionary board – Missions to the World – in Abidjan, a city of four million people on the Ivory Coast, when sixteen-year-old Muhammad walked into their centre and began asking questions about Christianity.

Muhammad, a Muslim, had become interested in Christ when one of his friends was converted. He had talked for hours with him, and came to John looking for answers to questions that his friend couldn't respond to. After talking with Muhammad for two or three hours, John gave him a French New Testament and sent him home.

Muhammad returned the next week with more questions. Towards the end of their conversation he became subdued, then said, 'John, there's something I need to talk about. That book you gave me is good [he had never seen the Bible]. But after reading it for only five minutes I become nauseated. I have to close it, and when I go to sleep I have nightmares and wake up feeling ill. Why?' As John listened to Muhammad he thought of what he had learned in a course, 'MC:510, The Miraculous and Church Growth,' that he had taken years earlier at Fuller Seminary. He thought Muhammad might be struggling with demonic influence in his life.

'Muhammad,' John asked, 'would you mind telling your story to some other Christians? I think they could help you.' Muhammad agreed, and John asked several recently converted Muslims to join them. After listening to Muhammad's story once more, John suggested that they pray for him. He consented.

What happened next was something John had never before personally dealt with on the mission field. Immediately after they began praying Muhammad's eyes rolled back into their sockets, he fell to the floor, and foam came out of his mouth. 'He looked unconscious. It was frightening.' After praying for about an hour, Muhammad 'came to', likening his experience to sticking his finger in a light socket. John was unsure at that time if Muhammad was delivered from the demon or demons that were tormenting him, so he told him to go home and memorise two verses and come back the next week for more counselling and prayer.

Over the next two months Muhammad met with John and several other believers every Thursday. Each week he received prayer and went home with two more verses to memorise. The prayer times continued to be dramatic; Muhammad was tormented by occultic practices, drug and alcoholic abuse, and a smoking habit. Towards the end of this period he put his faith in Christ, and his life was dramatically changed.

Muhammad's conversion was noticed back in his neighbourhood. His notorious reputation was transformed by God's grace; people wanted to know what had happened to him. Since his conversion Muhammad has led several people to Christ (no small accomplishment among Muslims), and he is teaching an area Bible study that John Weed hopes will some day become a church.

Demonic encounters are dramatic and bear great evangelistic fruit. Praying for the sick is another way of demonstrating the kingdom of God, as we will see in the next chapter.

25

POWER OVER DISEASE

One of Satan's most effective tools is disease. Almost half
of all the verses in the Gospels involve some form of power
encounter, with healing accounting for from 9 to 20 percent.[1] Yet too often we read these accounts through the
filters of modern scientism, assuming physical disease has
only a physical cause and solution. Subconsciously or consciously, when we read of healings in the New Testament
we assume that either they were only for the early Church
or there is another explanation – a scientific one – for how
these healings actually occurred. For this reason, for years
the only prayer for healing that I practised was, 'Lord,
guide the surgeon's hands.' I still pray that sometimes, but I
have many more options now.

Causes of disease may be physical, psychological or
spiritual. Regardless of the cause, though, Christians have
power over disease. Christians in the first century saw
disease as a work of Satan, a weapon of his demons, a way
in which evil rules the world. When Jesus healed disease,
whether demonically or physically caused, he pushed back
the kingdom of Satan. What the devil did, Jesus undid.

In Luke 13:10–17 we read of a woman crippled for
eighteen years who was healed by Jesus. Jesus called her
forward and said, 'Woman, you are set free from your
infirmity.' She had been incarcerated by Satan, and Jesus
was setting the captive free. 'Then he put his hands on her,
and immediately she straightened up and praised God.'

In response to attacks from the Pharisees (because Jesus

healed her on the Sabbath, a day of rest for the Jews), Jesus said, 'You hypocrites! . . . [S]hould not this woman, a daughter of Abraham, *whom Satan has kept bound for eighteen long years*, be set free . . .?' His was not a medical explanation. He identified the cause of her problem as Satan's doing. The Pharisees operated with hardness of heart and religious blindness. They hid behind theology, in this case the prohibition of work on the Sabbath.

*   *   *

During Christ's time, Edward Langton asserts in his book *Essentials of Demonology*, 'Special demons came to be associated with particular forms of disease or sickness. Certain diseases were held to be caused by particular demons.'[2] Again, not *all* cases of disease are caused by demons or are demons. Often, of course, there are psychological or physical explanations for illness. But more frequently than many Western Christians realise, the cause is demonic.

Seeing demons as a possible cause of disease is difficult to accept, because it challenges modern, materialistic notions about disease and infirmity. In Jesus' day, his explanation 'Satan has kept [her] bound' was accepted easily. Not even the Pharisees questioned it. Today, most Western people assume that her curvature of the spine was caused by an accident or developmental problem. Yet, whatever the means, Jesus thought Satan was the cause. We have been called to deal with the cause, not with how Satan inflicts disease and suffering.

Western Christians all too often look at disease and infirmity and accept it, saying, 'It must be the will of God' or 'We'll understand it better when we get to heaven.' In some cases God *doesn't* heal. But frequently people take these statements to mean God doesn't *want* to heal anyone today. In this sense, these statements are platitudes, falling short of what God has for us. He is a God of mercy and love and has given us the authority to do the works of Jesus.

*   *   *

In 1981, while in Johannesburg, South Africa, I was asked to pray over a fourteen-year-old Zulu boy who had not grown an inch since he was seven. His toes were partially missing; he suffered from a cleft palate and ruined teeth; he was incapable of speaking or walking (his mother carried him to the meeting). I was deeply saddened when I saw him.

When I spoke to him, he responded with incoherent mumblings. To get closer to him, I got down on my hands and knees. He looked up at me like a haunted animal – slobbering, mumbling, growling. His pupils rolled back in his head. He shrank back in terror when I spoke the name of Jesus. I knew then that I was dealing with a demon in him.

So I called over several other Christians, people whom I knew were experienced in deliverance, and we began praying over the boy. While praying, Becky Cook, an associate, discerned that a curse was on him. (She knew this through a word of knowledge; she had no previous knowledge of the boy or his family.) Someone had called demons on him when he was younger, asking them to torment and kill the boy. It was not clear at that time who had spoken the curse, but it seemed to be the source of his problems. We broke the power of the curse by speaking against it in the name of Christ, and then cast out several demons who were afflicting him.

Later we learned that when he was seven years old, living in another town, the boy had been a runner for a witch doctor, his aunt. His mother decided to move. Because the witch doctor was losing his service, she placed a curse on the child. The day the aunt placed the curse on the boy, the mother returned home to find him in a degenerated, animal-like condition. Over the years his condition had grown worse, until we encountered him in Johannesburg.

The results of breaking the curse were remarkable. Within two days, the boy returned to the meetings, walking and able to recognise me. His mother reported that he had made remarkable progress since we prayed for him. We prayed for him again that day, without much more progress. After we left South Africa, other Christians followed up with regular prayer. Four months later, he returned home (he had been institutionalised). He enrolled in school and in several months advanced two grade levels.

In Luke we find the story of Peter's mother-in-law's healing (Luke 4:38–9). Jesus, Scripture reports, 'rebuked the fever'. This is the same language that Jesus used to drive the demon out of the man in the synagogue at Capernaum. It may well be that the origin of the mother-in-law's fever was a demon. She was healed instantly. Jesus frequently spoke the same way to fevers as he did to demons, because he saw the connection between sickness and Satan.

*   *   *

Another tool for healing is God's forgiveness. When the paralytic was lowered through the roof in Capernaum, Jesus said, 'Son, your sins are forgiven' (Mark 2:5). In response to the Pharisees' attack on him for forgiving the paralytic's sins, Jesus asked, 'Which is easier: to say . . ., "Your sins are forgiven," or to say, "Get up, take your mat and walk"?' He then healed the paralytic. Obviously forgiveness of sins is a far greater miracle, for it opens the door to eternal life – the goal and purpose for signs and wonders.

There is great power in forgiveness of sin. In 1984 I spoke at a conference in the American Midwest. After one of the meetings, in the car park I met a woman who suffered with crippling arthritis. Her pain was so great that she needed a walking frame to get about. I talked with her before praying and discovered that her husband had abandoned her and her daughter fourteen years earlier, and it was shortly after this that her arthritic problems began. She also told me – and her daughter, who was with her – that her husband had run off with another man. She had kept this information from her daughter all these years.

On hearing this, I became enraged at what Satan had done and said, 'That's enough!' Here was an instance when the Holy Spirit stirred my heart, showing me that the source of this woman's arthritis was her yielding to bitterness towards her husband and God. I was angered by what Satan had done, and so was the Holy Spirit.

When I spoke those two words (they almost exploded out of me), the power of God fell on the woman. Her body trembled violently; her fingers and legs seemed to be straightened. Satan's grip, the power of bitterness and accusation, was broken. Then she confessed her sin of harbouring bitterness towards her husband and God. I reassured her of God's forgiveness. That night she was relieved of about 80 percent of her condition (swelling, pain, stiffness in the joints). More prayer was needed for the other 20 percent. (I know that she received more prayer; I do not know if she was completely restored.) Sin that finds safe harbour in our bodies is capable of all sorts of physical damage. Receiving and extending forgiveness was a key to her progress. On rare occasions Jesus demonstrated his power in an even more remarkable fashion, as we will see in the next chapter.

26

POWER OVER NATURE

Just as demonic forces cause havoc in the lives of men and women through sickness and demonisation, they can also exert their perverted influence in nature by causing it to run amok. In the fourth chapter of Mark's Gospel, Jesus waged war on 'a furious squall' and waves that threatened to swamp his and the disciples' boat as they crossed a lake. This story is often used to illustrate inward harmony for Christians as they encounter the various winds and waves of life's challenges. While this analogy may be a good one, it overlooks the primary intent of the author, which is to show Jesus ruling over nature itself.

Western materialists find Christ's rule over events in nature very difficult to accept. They see Christ's calming of the seas as a fantastic story smacking of animism and suggesting primitive religion, even superstition. The equating of *all* natural calamity with evil spirits would be animism, but simply acknowledging the possibility of Satan's influence in nature, and Christ's lordship over that influence, is not.

Christians also succumb to rationalism, thinking, 'Well, that's Christ's divinity ruling over natural forces – it doesn't relate to how we live today.' Yet the Bible teaches that Jesus performed miracles to demonstrate that he had the authority and power to do so, and that his power is available to us to do the same works.

The disciples in the boat were experienced fishermen. They knew the waters and what the storm could do; they thought that they were going to die. 'Teacher,' they said, 'don't you care if we drown?' After calming the storm, Jesus rebuked them for being afraid and lacking faith. Jesus' response used to puzzle me. Was not their fear reasonable, considering the circumstances? Then one day, while I was sitting beside the Sea of Galilee and meditating on this passage, the opening words of the text came to mind: 'He said to his disciples, "Let us go over to the other side."' The same person who said, 'Let there be light,' said, 'Let us go over to the other side.' When he asked, 'Do you still have no faith?' it was because he had already declared that they were going to the other side. The sure knowledge of the Father's will gave Jesus the liberty to sleep soundly while crossing, even during a storm. The disciples had to awaken him!

The words that Jesus used to calm the lake, 'Quiet! Be still!' are similar to those used to overcome demons and disease. He saw in nature's attack the work of Satan. This was a classic power encounter in which Jesus was at war with the perpetrator of destruction.

* * *

When I first began teaching my church congregation about this type of power encounter I had a humorous (and humbling) experience. In May 1982 I preached a series of sermons about the works of Jesus in nature. During the week between my third and fourth sermons I travelled to Denver, Colorado, where I had a speaking engagement.

Denver is called the 'Mile-High City', so named for its location over five thousand feet up in the majestic Rocky Mountains. Sudden spring storms with accumulations of twenty or more inches of snow are not unusual. On Thursday one of these storms hit the city, shutting down the airport and slowing road traffic. I decided to pray against the storm. For two days I prayed and nothing happened. The storm intensified. I was trapped in Colorado for the weekend.

That Sunday morning, back in sunny southern California, Bob Fulton, my co-pastor at the Vineyard Christian Fellowship, stood before the congregation and announced that I would not be preaching. 'A storm has hemmed John in the Rocky Mountains,' he said. 'He won't be able to tell us about the authority of Christ over nature.' I am told that it took several minutes before the laughter died down, and to this day church members occasionally remind me of the incident.

*   *   *

Not all stories of praying against storms end in failure. C. Peter Wagner reports a remarkable incident that occurred in September 1984 at a meeting in Stuttgart, Germany, of the Lausanne Committee on World Evangelisation. During the meeting the Committee received reports that hurricane Diana was about to slam into the southeastern coast of the United States, with the state of North Carolina taking the main blow. The reports were alarming; it was estimated that there could be great loss of life and property. Leighton Ford, president of the Lausanne Committee on World Evangelisation, owned a home in the anticipated path of the storm. He thought that he and many others could easily lose their homes.

'It was about 10:30 in the morning when we received word of Diana,' Dr Wagner now recalls. 'Right there, in the meeting, Kristy Mosvold of Norway suggested that I pray against it. So I stood up and began to pray, using the pattern of Christ's prayers against storms. Under what I felt as a special anointing of the Spirit I took authority over it, rebuking it.' Two hours later the Committee received word on the Armed Services Network that the hurricane had mysteriously stalled out at sea. Leighton Ford's home was spared. The next week *Newsweek* magazine ran an article in which meteorologists said Diana's sudden turn away from the coast was inexplicable. Later Diana returned and struck a glancing blow at the coast, but damage was minimal and nothing happened inland.

Perhaps what happened was a quirk of nature, the

explanation for which modern scientists do not yet have the technology to discern. But, based on Scripture, another plausible explanation is that God answered the Lausanne Committee's prayers, preventing the loss of many homes and lives, and sparing much suffering.

27

POWER OVER DEATH

'The end will come,' taught Paul, 'when [Jesus] hands over the kingdom to God the Father after he has destroyed all dominion, authority and power. For he must reign until he has put all his enemies under his feet. *The last enemy to be destroyed is death*' (1 Cor. 15:24–6). Jesus hated death – Satan's most fearful weapon – because it is the final result of sin.

Unlike delivering people from evil spirits, which Christ appeared to do every time he encountered a willing person, and healing, which he did with great frequency, resuscitation was infrequent. But the miracles of resuscitation – restoration to life of deceased persons – have enormous significance. Perhaps more than any other kind of miracle, they were a foretaste of the age to come, clear signals to Satan that his world was being invaded and overpowered by Jesus. The Gospels record three specific and one general account of his raising the dead.[1] These miracles strike Satan at his greatest point of strength and signal that his reign was broken by Jesus.

In Luke 7:11–17 Jesus raised from the dead a widow's son. Coming to the town of Nain, he encountered the widow's son's funeral procession. Luke wrote, 'When the Lord saw her, his heart went out to her and he said, "Don't cry."' He then commanded her son to get up. The crowd's response was to exclaim that 'God has come to help his people.'

Jesus is the embodiment of his Father, of the same

nature, functioning in perfect concert with his will for the redemption of the human race. The Father's will is to help people, to extend compassion and mercy. Resuscitation assured the people that God loved them, and that some day even death would be overcome.

* * *

The idea that Christ could raise someone from the dead *today* is difficult for many Western Christians to accept. Yet I have heard many reports (most of them from non-Western countries) of God working in this way.

For example, consider the story of Leslie Keegel, a Foursquare Church missionary who has worked in Sri Lanka since 1976. Sri Lanka's Buddhist culture has a reputation for being quite resistant to the gospel. Today, however, there are promising signs of both Buddhists and Hindus coming to Christ. The Foursquare Church has grown from a handful in the late 1970s to nearly nine thousand today, much of the growth coming from power evangelism. There is even one report of a raising from the dead. In 1982 Siripala and Winefreda, a middle-aged couple living in the Summitpura slums of Colombo, had an infant son who grew very ill. The worried parents called on Christian friends for help, but when they arrived the child was dead. Leslie Keegel eventually prayed for the child, and he was raised. Some forty extended family members received Jesus when they heard of his power and the gospel in raising Siripala and Winefreda's son from the dead.

* * *

Believing in the *possibility* of someone being raised from the dead today has an impact on Western Christians' faith and practice. However, stories like Leslie Keegel's are frequently received with scepticism. 'Why doesn't it happen closer to home?' are the words I frequently hear. I believe, though, that it does happen in Western society.

On 19 May 1985 at 3:30 p.m. eight-month-old Steven Christopher Dixon crawled out of a patio screen door that had been left open and fell into the family backyard swimming pool in Westminster, California. Some time later – the guesses range from fifteen to thirty minutes – his thirteen-year-old sister Gina discovered him in the water and screamed. Their father, Steven L. Dixon, came running.

'I pulled him out and immediately began CPR [cardiopulmonary resuscitation],' Dixon recalled. 'My wife, Dexcine, was at work, so I told Gina to call the paramedics.'

When the paramedics arrived, they found 'the child was very white', Captain Elvis Easley of the Westminster Fire Department reported. 'I saw a lot of fluid coming out of the baby's mouth.' Little Steven had no heartbeat and was, according to a published report in the *Los Angeles Times*, clinically dead. In the ambulance, a heart monitor recorded just a straight line, indicating no cardiac activity at all.

At the hospital a heart machine stimulated a slow heartbeat. Normally drowning victims who are submerged as long as Steven die or suffer severe brain damage. Dr Patrick Walsh, director of pediatric intensive care at the hospital, said, 'Close to zero will survive; 100 percent of the times that a victim is in full arrest, there is severe brain damage or death.' Walsh added that four to six minutes without oxygen is usually sufficient to cause severe brain damage.

Shortly after the child was taken to the hospital a friend of the family asked Josh Stewart, an associate pastor at the nearby Newport Vineyard, to come and pray for the baby. Dexcine Dixon was a Christian; her husband Steven was not. When Pastor Stewart arrived at the hospital the child's heart was still beating with aid of the heart machine. The doctor was not hopeful.

Dexcine asked Josh to pray for the child, and the doctor agreed. A nurse and family members watched as Josh laid his hands on Steven and quietly prayed, 'Give him back life. Allow there to be no brain damage or blindness. Bring back a normal heartbeat and brain function.' The prayer wasn't dramatic, and it only lasted three or four minutes, though Josh sensed God's presence. Josh then went home.

An hour later an excited Dexcine Dixon phoned Josh to tell him that a normal heartbeat and pulse had returned to Steven. A week later Steven returned home, completely normal. There was no brain damage, blindness or hearing loss.

It cannot be proved scientifically that Steven Christopher Dixon was raised from the dead. In fact, doctors at the hospital thought an unusual bodily reaction called hypothermia may have accounted for Steven's recovery. But hypothermia usually only happens in very cold water; it is rare in California because of higher water temperatures. 'That's what's so unusual about this case,' Dr Walsh admitted.

Steven L. Dixon, the baby's father, had a different explanation: 'It's phenomenal, a miracle. He was literally born again, and we thank God for that.' Dixon himself was born again that day, for through the experience he committed his life to Christ. 'It was God,' Dexcine Dixon later testified. 'God gave us a second chance. From the time he was found, right up to now, it was just the Lord's work.'

Study Session 6

DOING THE WORKS OF JESUS

Read *Power Evangelism*, Part Six, chapters 23–7, and *Power Healing*, chapters 4–7.

Purpose

Very few of us will ever raise the dead. But we will all deal with disease and demons in others. As Jesus' life demonstrates, healing the sick and demonised is integral to evangelism, a catalyst to great harvests. In this session you will look at how praying for the sick and confronting demons are related to evangelism.

Discussion

Have you had an opportunity in recent evangelistic encounters to pray for someone who was sick? Have you encountered demons in people? Have you ever had supernatural insights into people while you were sharing with them? Did these encounters result in conversions? Looking back on your recent evangelistic experiences, do you now recognise situations that could have been opportunities for power evangelism?

Plan of Action

Break up into groups of three or four and pray for each

other, asking the Holy Spirit to fill and empower you to pray for the sick, to cast out demons, to have supernatural insight, and – most important – to preach the gospel with boldness.

NAME	ENGEL SCALE	HOT ISSUES	PLAN OF ACTION
1.			
2.			
3.			
4.			
5.			
6.			
7.			
8.			
9.			
10.			

Now review and update your list of ten people from the previous week. Pray for them daily, asking God for the opportunity to share your testimony with one of them this week.

For Next Week

Come prepared to share your evangelistic experience with the group, with special concern to talk about your power encounter – should you have one.

Read *Power Evangelism*, Part Seven, chapters 28–31. Also, read *Power Healing*, chapters 11–12.

PART SEVEN

Signs and Wonders in the Church

28

CHRIST'S METHOD OF DISCIPLESHIP

When first-century Christians came to a new town, signs and wonders followed. Starting at Pentecost, power evangelism swept the Mediterranean, demonstrating that the kingdom of God had come. From Jerusalem to Rome, from Asia to Europe; among Jews, Samaritans and Gentiles; in every town, culture and race, God's rule was established. We should not be surprised at this: a major part of Christ's ministry was devoted to training the disciples to do the Father's works, to preparing them to lead the Church that was created at Pentecost.

But Christ's method of training is difficult for Western Christians to understand. There are several reasons for this. Evangelicals emphasise accumulating knowledge about God through Bible study. Christ was more action orientated; his disciples learned by doing as he did.

Scientific Bible study – specifically, the grammatical-historical study of Scripture – is the foremost, if not the exclusive, method of training among Western evangelicals today, especially in our seminaries. The grammatical-historical method employs history, linguistics and historical theology to discover what Scripture meant to its first-century audience. The method rightly assumes that what God intended to say to first-century Christians is what he intends for us also.

But there are problems related to the grammatical-historical method and the discipleship process. First, many seminary professors admit that reliance on an intellectual method within a classroom-orientated structure skews the goal of the discipleship process towards intellectual formation and away from moral and spiritual formation. As we shall see, Christ's method of training was rabbinic, more orientated towards learning a way of life through doing than through the accumulation of knowledge about God.

The second problem is that evangelicals tend to rely on this method alone for character formation. This leads to an intellectual understanding of Christianity. If the grammatical-historical method were used as one tool among many, there might not be the current tendency towards the intellectualisation of the Christian faith. But this is not usually the case.

As the New Testament scholar Russell P. Spittler says:

> The historical-critical method, when applied to Scripture, is both legitimate and necessary – but inadequate, . . . inadequate because . . . the end of biblical study cannot consist in historical dates or tentative judgments about complicated and conjectured literary origins. The end of biblical study consists rather in enhanced faith, hope, and love both for the individual and the community. The historical-critical method is inadequate, in other words, because it does not address piety.

For Spittler, an important element of piety is God speaking through Scripture and prayer.[1]

The last problem involves the effect the grammatical-historical method has on the process of Bible study. Scripture study needs to proceed in the spirit of faith, hope and love. By its nature, the grammatical-historical method is a rigorous intellectual task. The student easily falls into reliance on study rather than reliance on the Holy Spirit. Christ based his training on Scripture, and the goal of his training was piety, learning to hear God's voice and do his bidding.

Among Western Christians, another obstacle to understanding Christ's method of discipleship is the rejection of signs and wonders today. Signs and wonders, all Western evangelicals acknowledge, were necessary to authenticate Christ's divinity. Further, signs and wonders were a key factor in establishing the apostolic message of the Twelve and Paul. But most Western Christians reject or adopt a generally negative attitude towards signs and wonders after the first century. This diminishes the effectiveness of Christ's example for us and discounts much of what Christ intended that we do. What Christians – including evangelicals – are often left to follow is a good moral example, not a dynamic, Satan-conquering Lord. This results in overly intellectual disciples – certainly not a people who cause demons to tremble.

A closer look at how Jesus trained the disciples to do signs and wonders and how they carried on that ministry after Christ's ascension reveals many of the key elements for practising power evangelism today. That is the topic of the next chapter.

29

KEYS TO DISCIPLESHIP

Signs and wonders were the proof of Jesus' Messiahship, the calling cards of the kingdom of God. Their presence in the early Church demonstrates that Jesus intended them to be an integral part of the disciples' ministry.

The disciples learned from Jesus how to do the works of the kingdom. They might not have always understood the purpose of his miracles, but they learned how to do signs and wonders with remarkable success. Jesus' method of instruction was the method of the day: rabbinic. A rabbi would minister with his students watching; next they went out on short missions, reporting back for further instruction and correction from the master. After repeating this process for years, and when the rabbi was convinced his disciples were formed in *his* way of life, he released his students to become rabbis and teach others by the same process.

Christ used this same training method with his disciples. Christ, the Teacher, Rabbi, formed his disciples in *his* way of life, passing on his character. Faith, hope, love, joy, peace, and so on were the goals of his training. Performing signs and wonders – casting out demons, healing the sick, even walking on water – was the means by which the disciples learned more about God's nature. The disciples understood and accepted what Jesus expected of them. We never read of them objecting to being *asked* to do the works of Jesus, only of their sense of personal inadequacy in performing his commands.

*   *   *

In the early years of my upbringing I often visited a horse farm in Illinois where my grandfather worked. He trained Tennessee walking horses. Tennessee walkers have a remarkable high-strutting gait, different from any other horse in the world. One day I was with him while he worked on a horse with a problem gait. His solution was to hitch a pacer – a horse with the correct gait – to the horse with the problem and let them walk together. After a few days, the problem horse's gait became consistent, just like the pacer's. My grandfather explained that when a horse cannot do its job, if you connect it to one that can, soon both do the job correctly.

I have been training men and women for thirty-two years. During this period I have learned that the secret for success with people is the same as with horses: hitch a person who cannot do a job with one who can, and soon both will know how. This is how Christ trained the Twelve: they lived with him, soon living like him. Power evangelism works the same way. Being around someone who does it successfully is the best way to learn to do it yourself.

The primary criterion for becoming one of the Twelve was a willingness to follow Christ – to walk with him, and to choose to become like him. Other than that desire, the only thing the disciples had in common was that they were Jews with middle-class economic and social standing, living in Galilee. (Judas was the exception; the others were mostly fishermen.)

Through mutual commitment, Jesus made disciples out of the Twelve. He developed mature character and leadership in them. He trained them to do signs and wonders. They were hitched together for three years, and when released, the disciples continued to walk in his way. They performed signs and wonders and trained the next generation to perform them also.

But the disciples had difficulty in learning to do signs and wonders. They often misunderstood Christ's teachings (Matt. 13:36; 15:15; 16:6–12). They never fully understood his mission until the resurrection – and even then they were in need of further correction (Mark 8:31–2; 9:31–2; Acts 1:6). They also misunderstood his authority as it related to the kingdom of God (Mark 10:35–40; Luke 9:46–8). But Jesus was patient with them, for his goal was to build men who did the Father's bidding.

For three years, the Twelve were in a learning environment. They not only learned new ideas, they also developed new skills and abilities. They were teachable because they saw a large gap between Christ's life and their own. Progressive growth came through trial and error.

Frequent failures characterised the early ministry of all the disciples (Luke 9:37–43, 52–5), especially Peter's. His abortive attempt to walk on water (Matt. 14:25–33) is one of many examples. As the disciples continued to live with Christ, their failures diminished and their successes became more frequent. Each new step of faith was a springboard for their Master to push them further, enlarging their worldview and expanding their understanding of God.

*   *   *

Perhaps the most difficult lesson the disciples learned was how to have faith that results in miracles. Maybe I am overly sensitive to this because I had such difficulty learning about this type of faith. I think not, though.

For example, consider the feeding of the five thousand (Mark 6:33–44). This is one of the greatest miracles in the New Testament. Several points about faith can be learned from this episode that help with the practice of power evangelism.

First, Jesus was motivated by compassion. 'When Jesus landed and saw a large crowd, he had compassion on them, because they were like sheep without a shepherd.' Jesus' divine compassion, his supernatural mercy, frequently precipitated his works. (Moved by compassion, he healed, taught, performed miracles, raised the dead and expelled demons; see Matt. 20:34; Mark 1:41; 5:19; 6:34; 8:2–10; Luke 7:11–17.) We too need to ask God for his compassion.

Second, Jesus, listening to his Father, did not yield to the apostles' wish to send the crowd away. The apostles, observing the people's hunger and their lack of immediate resources, concluded that the crowd should be dispersed. Their solution was quite reasonable; they gave no thought to a miraculous provision. But if Jesus had acceded to their suggestion to disperse the crowd, one of the greatest miracles recorded in Scripture would have been lost. I wonder how many times we 'rationally and reasonably' miss miracles today? Jesus listened to the Father – not the disciples – and the miracle was performed.

Third, Jesus used the disciples' spiritual blindness on this occasion to train them in signs and wonders. 'You give them something to eat' is his response to their suggestion to disperse the crowd. This of course gave the apostles cause to re-examine their resources: five loaves and two fish. It was a crucial moment in their training. They were being told to do something for which they did not have adequate resources. I have discovered that praying for the healing of a blind person accomplishes the same thing in me. I know my own resources are inadequate. Miracles occur through our inadequacy, the crucible in which faith is formed.

Fourth, Jesus gave instructions to the disciples and they obeyed. He told them to organise the crowd 'in groups of hundreds and fifties'. They had no idea where the food was to come from; nevertheless, they prepared the people to receive. We are in the same position today: we need to listen to and act on Jesus' instructions, even when we cannot see the provision.

Finally, the miracle of multiplication of the bread and fish probably occurred in the apostles' hands as well as Christ's. He had commanded the apostles to 'give them something to eat'. Many commentators believe that the miracle of multiplication occurred only in the hands of Jesus. They may be correct, but the passage leaves room for thinking the miracle happened in the disciples' hands as well as Christ's – just as with exorcism and healing.

It is a possible interpretation that the apostles were

handed, after Christ's blessing, a meagre portion of bread and fish. Then they went into the crowd and began passing it out and the multiplication occurred before their eyes. The miracle was in their hands and hearts. They learned that multiplication could occur through them. Only God can work miracles, but he often does it by the hands of Christians.

We must do better than the apostles in learning from this miracle. Later, after Jesus walked on the water, Mark says 'They were completely amazed, for they had not understood about the loaves; their hearts were hardened' (Mark 6:51–2). Jesus had to show the Twelve again and again how to perform signs and wonders. With the help of the Holy Spirit and with soft hearts, we can avoid some of their failures.

30

COMMISSIONING MINISTRY

In Luke 9:1–2 we read: 'When Jesus had called the Twelve together, he gave them power and authority to drive out all demons and to cure diseases, and he sent them out to preach the kingdom of God and to heal the sick.' He was sending the disciples as his personal ambassadors; thus they went in his authority and power.

Their commissioning is analogous to being a train driver. Train drivers direct powerful machines, and success depends on working within specific schedules, on the right tracks, and at the proper speeds. Too often we think the authority and power of God is a *carte blanche* to do whatever we want, more like driving a car than a train. In fact, the commission to the Twelve came with stringent limitations: they were only to do the will of the Father.

When he sent them, Jesus provided the disciples with practical instructions (Matt. 10:5–20). He told them where and to whom they should go. They were to proclaim the kingdom of God to recipients, freely offering healing – no matter what the needs – because they themselves had received freely. A simple lifestyle of trusting God and owning few material possessions (for freedom of movement) was observed. They received hospitality and material support from people receptive to their message and avoided wasting time with those who rejected the kingdom. Persecution was expected, so they were taught to operate wisely yet keep their innocence (not an easy task, though

Christ's life was their pattern). In all instances Jesus' Spirit would help instruct them.

Even though given the authority and power of the kingdom of God, the Twelve still had to exercise it. Power, I too have learned, comes as we exercise what God has given. The disciples could give only what they had received, but in giving they received more. Until they actually healed the sick and cast out demons, their authority and power meant little to them.

The Twelve encountered difficulties, though at first their excursions were successful – even the demons were subject to them! Soon, however, they faced difficulties with their own pride and carnality. For example, they tried to stop others who were healing in Jesus' name, and they lapsed into unbelief. They also experienced persecution from religious leaders.

In Luke 9:41, we read of Christ's response to the disciples' failure, in this case their inability to cast a demon from a child: 'O unbelieving and perverse generation, how long shall I stay with you and put up with you?' Jesus was frustrated with their lack of faith. It was very important to him that they learn how to cast out all demons, so when he departed from earth that ministry would continue.

Christ delivered the boy of the evil spirit immediately, using the occasion to teach the disciples that soon they would not have his help. 'Listen carefully to what I am about to tell you: The Son of Man is going to be betrayed into the hands of men' (Luke 9:44). They needed to learn about faith for deliverance, because he was soon to leave them.

Signs and wonders were done through the followers' faith, quickened by the guidance of the Holy Spirit. When with Jesus, the disciples were trained in faith for miracles. When Peter and John healed the lame man at the gate called Beautiful, Peter explained that it was not because of their spirituality; faith in Jesus' name made the man whole (Acts 3:1–10). This assertive faith has confidence without need of proof or regard for evidence, a willingness to stand by what God commands. (I do not imply that we claim someone is healed when symptoms of illness are still present. Faith for healing means that we believe God is able to heal specific persons today and there is a specific sense of God's working.)

The expansion of the ministry of signs and wonders from the One to many has cosmic effects. When Jesus sent out the Twelve, and later the Seventy-two, he increased the possibilities for people's deliverance from the devil. The kingdom of darkness suffered defeat. The expansion of the kingdom of God – and accompanying defeat of Satan – is affected by the number of Christians performing signs and wonders.

31

TRANSFERRING MINISTRY

For three years Jesus taught the disciples how to minister from hearts of compassion and mercy, hear the Father, grow in dependence on the Holy Spirit, be obedient to God's leading, and believe that God performs miracles through men and women. Even though they frequently forgot or misunderstood what they were taught, his post-resurrection commission, as recorded in Mark 16:14–20, was consistent with their training:

> Jesus appeared to the Eleven as they were eating; he rebuked them for their lack of faith . . . [and he] said to them, 'Go into all the world and preach the good news to all creation . . . And these signs will accompany those who believe: In my name they will drive out demons; they will speak in new tongues; they will pick up snakes with their hands; and when they drink deadly poison, it will not hurt them at all; they will place their hands on sick people, and they will get well.'
> . . . Then the disciples went out and preached everywhere, and the Lord worked with them and confirmed his word by the signs that accompanied it.

I find it remarkable that many Western Christians are surprised at the emphasis on signs and wonders in this commissioning. Yet the way the disciples fulfilled the great commission indicates Christ's commitment to power evangelism, a key part of their training.

Some have challenged the genuineness of Mark 16:9–20.

While it is true that several of the most reliable early manuscripts do not contain this passage, all Christian traditions have included it in the canon of Scripture. But even if the passage is excluded from the canon, we cannot disregard the overwhelming evidence that the early disciples in fact fulfilled the Markan commission: they cast out demons, spoke in tongues, picked up snakes, and healed the sick. If the passage was not in the original text, another question arises: Why was such a text added – if it was, as evidence suggests (*not* confirms) – in the second century?

Luke was the theologian of the Holy Spirit. In the first chapter of Acts, he wrote that Acts was a companion volume to his Gospel. The purpose of his Gospel was to write all that Jesus did and taught (Acts 1:1). In Acts, Luke continued the story of Jesus' works and teaching, only now it was done by the disciples (Acts 1:8).

Luke began the book of Acts by contrasting the disciples before Pentecost with the empowered group after. In Acts 1, the disciples still operated according to Old Testament principles. They misunderstood Christ's mission (Acts 1:6); they chose Judas' replacement by casting lots, recalling the Urim and Thummim of the Old Testament (Exod. 28:30). After the Spirit came, when someone needed to be chosen to fill an office, they used different methods (see Acts 6:1–6). The training they received in discipleship came together with the catalytic outpouring of God's Spirit at Pentecost. Power evangelism was unleashed on the world.

As I pointed out in chapter 12, there are at least ten kinds of sign phenomena in the book of Acts that produced evangelistic growth in the Church. The following is a summary of the types of phenomena in Acts:

Speaking gifts. Tongues and prophecy occur four times in Acts, as a result of three of which the church grew. For example, at Pentecost the disciples were 'filled with the Holy Spirit and began to speak in other tongues as the Spirit enabled them', resulting in 'about three thousand [being] added to their number that day' (2:4, 41).[1]

Visions. There are four instances of visions. Cornelius, the Caesarean centurion, received a vision – an answer to his prayers – and was told to send for Peter. The next day, Peter had a related vision. The two visions resulted in the gospel being preached to the Gentiles for the first time, with many responding by being baptised (see 10:1, 3, 9, 47).[2]

Dead raised. Two resuscitations are recorded. The first is Dorcas (or Tabitha, as she was called in Aramaic); Peter raised her from the dead, resulting in 'many people [believing] in the Lord' (9:40–2). The second is Eutychus, raised from the dead by Paul, with no recorded evangelistic result (20:7–12).

Assorted miracles. There are six specific miracles recorded. On the island of Malta a viper bit Paul and he suffered no ill effects. According to church tradition, the people responded to the miracle by believing in Christ, and the church was established (28:3–10).[3]

There were also phenomena that were likened to miracles of nature. For example, the opening of the gates for Peter in Acts 12; the earthquake, unfastened fetters, and opened doors in Acts 16; and the sound like wind and tongues like fire in Acts 2. The last phenomenon helped account for three thousand converts (Acts 2:41).

Healings. There are seven specific healings. Peter healed Aeneas' paralysis, resulting in the conversion of the towns of Lydda and Sharon (Acts 9:32–5).[4]

Angelic visitations. There are three recorded visitations. An angel told Philip to go to a desert road south of Jerusalem; there he evangelised the Ethiopian eunuch (Acts 8:26–40). According to church tradition, the eunuch returned to Ethiopia and established the church.[5]

What conclusions can be drawn from my brief survey of the book of Acts? First, the early Church – particularly the Twelve – carried on Christ's ministry, and this included signs and wonders. They were trained by Christ in how to do them, and they did them well. Second, not only the Twelve healed the sick, cast out demons, and experienced visions. Other Christians did too. Signs and wonders were a part of daily life, expected by the Church. Paul, Stephen, Cornelius, Ananias – none of them members of the original Twelve – all practised signs and wonders. Finally, signs and wonders resulted in dramatic church growth. They were a catalyst for evangelism.

Study Session 7

TRANSFERRING MINISTRY

Read *Power Evangelism*, Part Seven, chapters 28–31.

Purpose

In this session you will explore how Jesus trained the Twelve and what implications that has for us in power evangelism. Your goal will be to have greater commitment and confidence to practise power evangelism.

Discussion

Look back over the last six weeks and ask these questions:

1. Am I more conscious of the calling to evangelise?
2. Am I now actually sharing the gospel with people? With more people than before we began the study?
3. Do I see power demonstrations like healing and casting out demons as an integral part of evangelism?
4. Have I actually prayed for a person's illness or attempted to confront a demon? What were the results?
5. Am I more conscious of divine appointments? Have I kept some dramatic appointments?
6. Do I have greater faith for miracles?

Suggestions for Sharing this Week

Never:

- Raise a laugh at anybody's expense.
- Attempt to win an argument. (God's word needs no defence.)
- Force a person to admit that he or she is wrong.
- Aim at a person's emotions. (Truth should make its own appeal.)
- Use too much Christian jargon, such as 'saved', 'convicted', 'washed in the blood', and so on.
- Speak critically about another individual, church, or group.

Always:

- Avoid arguments.
- Aim for real, genuine dialogue.
- Be a good listener. (Do not interrupt!)
- Ask God for wisdom as you are sharing.
- Be honest and say if you do not know something.

Remember:

- God keeps our appointment book.
- Most people need to hear the gospel many times before they believe in Christ.
- All questions about God will tend to be the same, regardless of the socio-economic group the seeker comes from.
- We cannot force our point of view, but we can teach.
- When we answer people's questions, they are attentive listeners.
- The ultimate goal is for people to believe in Christ, but your immediate goal may be to nudge them along the Engel Scale, closer to conversion.

Plan of Action

The following is a system for personal evangelism that I developed years ago. It's a tool for focusing your prayers and actions on personal evangelism, a daily reminder of our calling to reach out with the gospel. (You may photocopy this page for your use.)

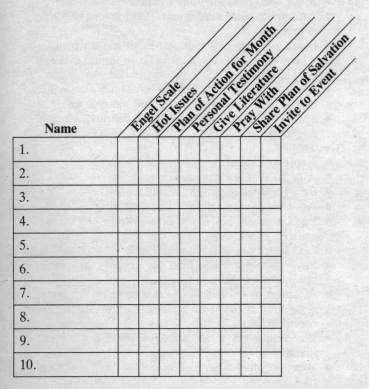

	Engel Scale	Hot Issues	Plan of Action for Month	Personal Testimony	Give Literature	Pray With	Share Plan of Salvation	Invite to Event
Name								
1.								
2.								
3.								
4.								
5.								
6.								
7.								
8.								
9.								
10.								

Using the list of people that you have been praying for and reaching out to over the past five weeks, fill in the ten (or more) spaces above and then, over the course of each month, write in the *date* that you accomplish each task.

At the end of the month you can transfer the names of people you feel led to continue reaching out to, and add new names of people God brings into your life. The most important space is the plan of action for that month. Pray through what you think God wants for each person, and then pray daily to fulfil that purpose.

Afterword

WHAT SHALL I DO?

In 1981 I was invited to preach at St Andrew's Anglican Church in Chorleywood, Hertfordshire, England. David Watson and Eddie Gibbs had encouraged Bishop David Pytches, the vicar of St Andrew's, to invite me to speak. He consented, inviting me for two days, a Saturday morning to Sunday evening.

St Andrew's is a suburban church composed mostly of professionals, including members of the House of Commons, doctors, lawyers, and educators. The pastor before David Pytches had introduced St Andrew's to the charismatic renewal, which most of the members received, though in a fairly subdued fashion. St Andrew's was and is a 'properly Anglican' congregation; I was apprehensive about how the people would respond to teaching about signs and wonders.

On Saturday morning I taught about church growth, introducing them to the relationship between the miraculous and growing churches. That evening I spoke on healing, seeing only a moderate response when I prayed over people at the end of the session.

By Sunday morning the church was buzzing with talk about the power of God, some of the people being upset with what I said and did the previous evening. After the Eucharist liturgy, my associates and I again prayed over people. My brother-in-law, Bob Fulton, prayed over a woman who was blind in one eye. When she told Bob what her problem was, he heard her incorrectly, thinking that she had said, 'I have arthritis.' So he prayed for her to be healed of arthritis (which she didn't have), but the result was her receiving sight. Her response was to begin yelping – something not well received by many in the congregation. Bob almost fainted. By Sunday afternoon David Pytches' phone was ringing off the hook; people were calling to express concern about what they thought were excesses.

That evening I became concerned about how the congregation was receiving what I had said. But when the evening service began I sensed the powerful presence of the Holy Spirit. Before we left many people were healed and, so it was later reported to me, as many as one hundred young people gave their lives to God that evening or immediately after. Many of them are today preparing for the ministry. To that date, it was the most powerful meeting outside of Vineyard Christian Fellowship gatherings that I had conducted.

David Pytches' response throughout the weekend was joy and laughter, although neither he nor I fully understood what God was doing. As I left on the Monday morning, his last words, spoken in a mocking dismay, were, 'You've torn my church into bits and pieces. What shall I do?'

'What shall I do?' How many times I have heard that question after people have experienced the kingdom of God and tasted the Holy Spirit. When I finish teaching the last session of the course 'The Miraculous and Church Growth' at Fuller Seminary, I am often approached by students asking how what I have taught is meant to work in their churches. Over half of my students are pastors or missionaries home on furlough, so for them, as for David Pytches, this is a pressing concern.

*   *   *

Several years ago a Methodist pastor who had recently taken the signs and wonders course at Fuller Seminary wrote to me asking for advice. On the verge of retirement, he had initially enrolled in the course to gain credits that would improve his denominational pension. But by the end of the term his life was changed – he had been empowered with the Holy Spirit and it had radically changed his outlook towards the ministry.

'John,' he wrote, 'I serve on countless committees and do an endless amount of administration. I want to minister in the power of God, but how can I if I'm always going to district meetings, financial committees, and other sorts of bureaucratic gatherings?'

My advice to him was simple: It does not matter where you are but what you are. Like Jesus, we are called to do the Father's bidding wherever he has placed us. Instead of looking to change things outwardly, I cautioned him, we should let God change us inwardly.

Later I heard back from him. 'John,' he wrote, 'I took your advice. Now I go to committee meetings and ask God to lead me to meet people's needs, to show me what he wants me to say and do. Rarely does a session go by where I do not pray over another pastoral leader or committee member. Further, wherever I go I am always asking the Father to show me his will so I can do his works.'

The pastor explained how when he asked people how they were and they told him their problems, he prayed over them, with excellent results. He did not go into a long explanation with the people about what he was doing, he simply did it.

This is the way most of the members of the Vineyard Christian Fellowship go about their daily lives. One member of our church, Keith Endow, is an estate agent who regularly prays over clients who have needs. And they never complain, because the Holy Spirit always comes on them. For example, several years ago he was showing a client through the home of an elderly couple who were moving due to the recent divorce of a daughter. All around their home were photographs and paintings of their daughter, son-in-law, and grandchildren. The couple were moving to help their daughter through a difficult time. So, just before leaving, Keith told them he was a Christian and asked if he could pray for them. They readily accepted and the Holy Spirit brought a peace and blessing to them.

It is important that we are where God wants us to be. Yet I am convinced that Christians frequently use their situation in life as an excuse for not being used by God right now; that they too often think if only they were in the 'right place' they could do the types of things I have described in this book.

* * *

Another question people frequently ask is, 'Under whom can I get discipled in power evangelism? Who will teach me how to do it?'

I do not discount the need for practical discipleship, the need to learn from older and more experienced brothers and sisters in all areas of Christian living. But when I hear people asking this question, sometimes I wonder if they are by-passing the only true discipler: Jesus. He made the first disciples, and he has continued to make disciples, down through the centuries. But too often we allow humans to take his place, missing out on the opportunity to receive his Lordship in our heart. We should read good Christian literature, go to conferences, and learn from those who are effective at what I have described in this book, but we should beware of allowing human leaders to take the place of God.

* * *

Finally, we must learn to wait on God, allowing him to speak, act, lead – always yielding our right to control whatever situation we are in. There is something very simple, almost childlike, about power evangelism. God gives impressions, and we act on them. If he does not speak to us, then we wait – something difficult for action-orientated Western people to do.

This is a simple faith, the kind that Jesus cultivated in the disciples: he always looked for responsive people, men and women who acted on his words, even when they did not understand the words' ramifications (which was often the case). 'Come, follow me' was all it took for most of the disciples to leave everything behind and follow the kingdom of God. Our call is no different today.

When the cloudburst of the Holy Spirit came on the disciples at Pentecost, when they were drenched with his power, the key to their success remained the same: emptying themselves from all desire to control God, yielding their lives in service to him.

What should we do? David Pytches stayed at St Andrew's, not creating radical organisational changes, but encouraging the people to open their hearts to God, walk in his power, and obey his voice. He watched St Andrew's become a greater source of spiritual renewal and evangelism in the United Kingdom. We might be homemakers, factory workers, secretaries, salespersons or teachers, but we all have the same challenge as David Pytches and the people of St Andrew's: to yield control of our lives to the Holy Spirit, learning to hear and do his will, risking all we have to defeat Satan and to advance the kingdom of God.

APPENDIX A
SIGNS AND WONDERS IN
CHURCH HISTORY

Though only a sampling, the following material documents signs and wonders through the centuries. I have limited my sources to major personalities and movements, with a few illustrations of lesser-known people. For further reading and documentation, I refer you to the Bibliography.

I separated church history into three ages: patristic, medieval, and Reformation-modern. The twentieth century warrants a separate treatment, found in Appendix B.

The Patristic Era, 100–600

JUSTIN MARTYR (c. 100–65)
Justin was a Christian apologist who had studied all the great philosophies of his day. In his *Second Apology* (c. 153), Justin, in speaking about the names, meaning, and power of God and Christ, writes concerning exorcism and healing:

> For numberless demoniacs throughout the whole world, and in your city, many of our Christian men exorcising them in the name of Jesus Christ, who was crucified under Pontius Pilate, have healed and do heal, rendering helpless and driving the possessing devils out of the men, though they could not be cured by all the other exorcists, and those who used incantations and drugs. (Coxe 6:190)

In his *Dialogue with Trypho* (a learned Jew), Justin refers to the current use of spiritual gifts:

For the prophetical gifts remain with us, even to the present time. And hence you ought to understand that [the gifts] formerly among your nation have been transferred to us. (Coxe 1:240)

. . . I have already said, and do again say, that it has been prophesied that this would be done by Him after His ascension to heaven. It is accordingly said, 'He ascended on high, He led captivity captive, He gave gifts unto the sons of men.' And again, in another prophecy, it is said 'And it shall come to pass after, I will pour out My Spirit on all flesh, and on My servants, and on My handmaids, and they shall prophesy.' Now, it is possible to see amongst us women and men who possess gifts of the Spirit of God . . . (Coxe 1:243)

IRENAEUS (140–203)

Irenaeus was the Bishop of Lyons. His five books *Against Heresies* are devoted to the heresy of Gnosticism. In refuting it he says:

For some do certainly and truly drive out devils, so that those who have thus been cleansed from evil spirits frequently join themselves to the Church. Others have foreknowledge of things to come: they see visions, and utter prophetic expressions. Others still, heal the sick by laying their hands upon them, and they are made whole. Yea, moreover, as I have said, the dead even have been raised up, and remained among us for many years. And what shall I more say? It is not possible to name the number of gifts which the Church, [scattered] throughout the whole world, has received from God, in the name of Jesus Christ.

TERTULLIAN (c. 160/170–215/220)

Not many details are known concerning Tertullian's life. He was reared in the cultured paganism of Carthage. He became a Christian and joined the Montanist group about 206. He was a prolific writer. In his work *To Scapula*, chapter 5, he gives this account of expelling demons and healing:

> All this might be officially brought under your notice, and by the very advocates, who are themselves also under obligations to us, although in court they give their voice as it suits them. The clerk of one of them who was liable to be thrown upon the ground by an evil spirit, was set free from his affliction; and was also the relative of another, and the little boy of a third. How many men of rank (to say nothing of common people) have been delivered from devils, and healed of diseases! Even Severus himself, the father of Antonine, was graciously mindful of the Christians; for he sought out the Christian Proculus, surnamed Torpacion, the steward of Euhodias, and in gratitude for his having once cured him by anointing, he kept him in his palace till the day of his death. (Coxe 3:107)

NOVATIAN (210–80)

Novatian of Rome is noted for two reasons: he was the antipope of the puritan party in the Church, and he gave the Western Church its first full-length treatment of the Trinity. In chapter 29 of his *Treatise Concerning the Trinity* he writes of the Spirit:

> This is He who places prophets in the Church, instructs teachers, directs tongues, gives powers and healings, does wonderful works, offers discrimination of spirits, affords powers of government, suggests counsels, and orders and arranges whatever other gifts there are of *charismata*; and thus makes the Lord's Church everywhere, and in all, perfected and completed. (Coxe 5:641)

ANTONY (c. 251–356)

Our knowledge of Antony depends largely on his biography, written by Athanasius. Chapter 40 of this biography shows Antony's work with the supernatural, especially in dealing with demons:

Once, a very tall demon appeared with a procession of evil spirits and said boldly: 'I am the power of God, I am His providence. What do you wish that I grant you?' I then blew my breath at him, calling on the name of Christ, and I tried to strike him. I seemed to have succeeded, for, immediately, vast as he was, he and all his demons disappeared at the name of Christ.

HILARION (c. 291–371)

Hilarion was an ascetic, educated and converted at Alexandria. By the time he had been in the desert for twenty-two years, he became widely known by reputation throughout the cities of Palestine. Jerome in his *Life of Saint Hilarion* tells of a number of the miracles, healings, and expulsions of demons that occurred during his ministry:

> Facidia is a small suburb of Rhinoocorura, a city of Egypt. From this village, a woman who had been blind for ten years was brought to be blessed by Hilarion. On being presented to him by the brothers (already there were many monks with him), she told him that she had bestowed all her substance on physicians. To her the saint replied: 'If what you lost on physicians you had given to the poor, Jesus the true Physician would have healed you.' Whereupon she cried aloud and implored him to have mercy on her. Then, following the example of the Saviour, he rubbed spittle upon her eyes and she was immediately cured. (15:254–5)

Jerome concludes the section he devoted to telling of Hilarion's life by stating, 'There would not be time if I wanted to tell you all the signs and wonders performed by Hilarion . . .' (15:262–3).

MACRINA THE YOUNGER (c. 328–79/80)

Macrina was the sister of Basil, Bishop of Caesarea, and also of Gregory, Bishop of Nyssa. Gregory tells of the following healing:

There was with us our little girl who was suffering from an eye ailment resulting from an infectious sickness. It was a terrible and pitiful thing to see her as the membrane around the pupil was swollen and whitened by the disease.

I went to the men's quarters where your brother Peter was Superior, and my wife went to the women's quarters to be with St Macrina. After an interval of time we were getting ready to leave but the blessed one would not let my wife go, and said she would not give up my daughter, whom she was holding in her arms, until she had given them a meal and offered them 'the wealth of philosophy'. She kissed the child as one might expect and put her lips on her eyes and, when she noticed the diseased pupil she said, 'If you do me the favour of remaining for dinner I will give you a return in keeping with this honour.' When the child's mother asked what it was, the great lady replied, 'I have some medicine which is especially effective in curing eye disease.'

We gladly remained and later started the journey home, bright and happy. Each of us told his own story on the way. My wife was telling everything in order, as if going through a treatise, and when she came to the point at which the medicine was promised, interrupting the narrative, she said, 'What have we done? How did we forget the promise, the medicine for the eyes?'

I was annoyed at our thoughtlessness, and quickly sent one of my men back to ask for the medicine, when the child, who happened to be in her nurse's arms, looked at her mother, and the mother, fixing her gaze on the child's eyes said, 'Stop being upset by our carelessness.' She said this in a loud voice, joyfully and fearfully. 'Nothing of what was promised to us has been omitted, but the true medicine that heals diseases, the cure that comes from prayer, this she has given us, and has already worked; nothing at all is left of the disease of the eyes.'

As she said this, she took our child and put her in my arms, and I also then comprehended the miracles in the gospel which I had not believed before, and I said, 'What a great thing it is for sight to be restored to the blind by the hand of God, if now his handmaiden makes such cures and has done such a thing through faith in him, a fact no less impressive than these miracles.'

AMBROSE (c. 339–97)

Ambrose was the Bishop of Milan. When ordained as a bishop his first act was to distribute his wealth among the poor. He was an outstanding preacher and teacher and very outspoken.

Ambrose in *The Holy Spirit (Fathers of the Church)* states that healings and tongues were still given by God:

Behold, the Father established the teachers; Christ also established them in the churches; and just as the Father gives the grace of healings, so the Son also gives it; just as the Father gives the gift of tongues, so the Son also has bestowed it. (Deferrari 44:150)

AUGUSTINE (354–430)

Augustine was Bishop of Hippo and the greatest of the Latin Fathers. He was baptised by Ambrose in Milan at Easter 387.

At the close of his life, he wrote *The City of God* (c. 413–27). In book 22, chapter 28, Augustine details the miracles that were occurring in his day: 'It is sometimes objected that the miracles, which Christians claimed to have occurred, no longer happen.' He argues that the ones that happened and were recorded in the New Testament are 'absolutely trustworthy'. Then he writes, 'The truth is that even today miracles are being wrought in the name of Christ, sometimes through His sacraments and sometimes through the intercession of the relics of his saints.'

Augustine then tells of the miracles that happened (Deferrari 24:431–45).

A blind man whose sight was restored (24:433)

The Bishop Innocent of Carthage healed of a rectal fistula (24:433–7)

Innocentia in Carthage healed of breast cancer (24:437–8)

A doctor in Carthage healed of gout (24:438–9)

An ex-showman of Curcubis healed of paralysis and a hernia in the scrotum (24:439)

The healing of Hesperius, one of Augustine's neighbours, whose diseases were caused by 'evil spirits' (24:439)

A demonised boy cured, after the demon ripped out his eye and left it 'hanging by a tiny vein as by a root. The pupil which was black, turned white' (24:440–1)

A young girl in Hippo delivered from demons (24:441)

Florentius of Hippo who prayed for money and received it (24:441–2)

A blind woman healed in Hippo (24:442)

Bishop Lucillus of Synity healed of a fistula (24:442–3)

Eucharius, a Spanish priest, possibly brought back from the dead (24:443)

Martila who was healed and saved (24:443–4)

Three healed of gout (24:444)

A child, who was run over by a cart, healed with no sign of being run over (24:444)

The resuscitation of a nun (24:444)

The resuscitation of a Syrian's daughter (24:444)

Augustine's friend's son who was raised from the dead (24:445)

Augustine ends his narrative of miracles by telling his readers that there are too many miracles to list. 'It is a simple fact', Augustine writes, 'that there is no lack of miracles even in our day. And the God who works the miracles we read of in the scriptures uses any means and manner he chooses.'

GREGORY OF TOURS (c. 538–94)
Gregory was a bishop and historian. He was a prolific

writer, whose works provide invaluable knowledge of sixth-century church life (Douglas 1974: 436). There are many accounts of healings that occurred in Gregory's time. They are to be found in his *Dialogues*, where he also relates the expelling of a demon and his own healing:

Eleutherius, whom I mentioned previously, abbot of the Monastery of St. Mark, the Evangelist adjoining the walls of Spoleto, lived with me for a long time in my monastery at Rome and died there. His disciples say that he raised a dead person to life by the power of his prayer. He was well known for his simplicity and compunction of heart, and undoubtedly through his tears this humble, childlike soul obtained many favours from almighty God.

I will tell you about a miracle of his which I had him describe to me in his own simple words. Once while he was travelling, evening came on before he could find a lodging for the night, so he stopped at a convent. There was a little boy in this convent who was troubled every night by an evil spirit. So, after welcoming the man of God to their convent, the nuns asked him to keep the boy with him that night. He agreed, and allowed the boy to rest near him. In the morning the nuns asked him with deep concern whether he had done anything for the boy. Rather surprised that they should ask, he said, 'No.' Then they acquainted him with the boy's condition, informing him that not a night passed without the evil spirit troubling the boy. Would Eleutherius please take him along to the monastery because they could no longer bear to see him suffer? The man of God agreed to do so.

The boy remained a long time in the monastery without being troubled in the least. Highly pleased at this, the old abbot allowed his joy at the boy's healthy condition to exceed moderation. 'Brothers,' he said to his monks, 'the Devil had his joke with the sisters, but once he encountered real servants of God, he no longer dared to come near this boy.' That very instant, hardly waiting for

Eleutherius to finish speaking, the Devil again took possession of the young boy, tormenting him in the presence of all. The sight of it filled the old man's heart with grief, and when his monks tried to console him he said, 'Upon my word! Not one of you shall taste bread today until this boy is snatched out of the Devil's power.'

He prostrated himself in prayer with all his monks and continued praying until the boy was freed from the power of the evil spirit. The cure was complete and the Devil did not dare molest him any further.

GREGORY I (THE GREAT) (540–604)

Gregory the Great was pope from 590 to 604. His *Dialogues* (593–4) were described by the author himself as stories of 'the miracles of the Fathers which were done in Italy'. The *Dialogues* contain supernatural tales, which divide neatly into three classes: stories of visions, stories of prophecies, and stories of miracles.

The following, a summary of one of Gregory's stories, is taken from Frederick Dudden's seminal work on the life of Gregory:

One day at Subiaco, the little monk Placidus, the future Apostle of his [Gregory's] Order in Sicily, went to the lake to draw water, but overbalanced himself and fell in. Benedict, who was sitting in his cell, was supernaturally aware of the occurrence, and cried out hastily to his disciple Maurus: 'Run, Brother Maurus, for the child who went to fetch water has fallen into the lake, and the stream has carried him a great way.' Maurus ran down to the edge of the lake, and then, 'thinking still that he went on dry land, he ran on the water', caught the drifting boy by the hair and brought him safely back. It was only when he stood again on the firm ground that Maurus realised that a miracle had taken place, and 'much astonished, he wondered how he had done that which knowingly he would not have dared to venture'. (Dudden, vol. 1, 1905: 334)

The Medieval Era, 600–1500

St Francis of Assisi (1181–1226)

St Francis was the founder of the Franciscan order. He had an extensive healing ministry. The following selections are taken from a vast number of miracles that occurred in the ministry of Francis:

> Once when the holy man of God Francis was going about through various regions to preach the kingdom of God, he came to a certain city called Toscanella. There, when he was sowing the seed of life in his usual way, a certain soldier of that city gave him hospitality; he had an only son who was lame and weak of body. Though he was a young child, he had passed the years of weaning; still he remained in a cradle. When the father of the boy saw the great sanctity of the man of God, he humbly cast himself at his feet, begging from him health for his son. But Francis, who considered himself useless and unworthy of such great power and grace, refused for a long time to do this. But finally overcome by the insistence of his petitions, he prayed and then put his hand upon the boy and, blessing him, raised him up. Immediately, with all present looking on and rejoicing, the boy arose completely restored and began to walk here and there about the house.

> Once when the man of God Francis had come to Narni and was staying there for a number of days, a certain man of that city, Peter by name, lay in bed paralysed. For a period of five months he had been so deprived of the use of all his limbs that he could not rise at all or move himself even a little; and thus having completely lost the use of his feet and hands and head, he could only move his tongue and open his eyes. When he heard that Francis had come to Narni, he sent a messenger to the bishop of that city to ask him for the love of God to send the servant of the most high God to him, confident that he would be freed from the illness from which he suffered at the sight and presence of Francis. And so it happened

that, when the blessed Francis had come to him and had made the sign of the cross over him from his head to his feet, he was immediately healed and restored to his former health. (Hermann n.d.: 59–60)

WALDENSIAN COMMUNITY

This was a movement in the Middle Ages whose characteristics included evangelical obedience to the gospel, rigorous asceticism, aversion to recognising the ministry of unworthy priests, belief in visions, prophecies, and spirit possession (Douglas 1974: 1026). A. J. Gordon in his book *The Ministry of Healing* quotes the following doctrine of the Waldensians:

Therefore, concerning this anointing of the sick, we hold it *as an article of faith*, and profess sincerely from the heart that sick persons, when they ask it, may lawfully be anointed with the anointing oil by one who joins them in praying that it may be efficacious to the healing of the body according to the design and end and effort mentioned by the apostles; and we profess that such an anointing performed according to the apostolic design and practice will be healing and profitable. (Gordon 1802: 65)

VINCENT FERRER (1350–1419)

Vincent was a Dominican preacher who was born in Valencia. Known as the 'Angel of the Judgement', he preached across Europe for almost twenty years. The *New Catholic Encyclopedia* records the following:

Vincent was disillusioned; he became gravely ill. In a vision, he was commissioned by the Lord, who was accompanied by St. Dominic and St. Francis, 'to go through the world preaching Christ.' After a year had passed Benedict permitted him to go. In November 1399, therefore, he set forth from Avignon and spent 20 years in apostolic preaching. As the spirit moved him or as he was requested, he visited and revisited places

throughout Spain, southern France, Lombardy, Switzerland, northern France, and the Low Countries. With
fiery eloquence he preached the need of repentance and
the coming of the Judgment. He seldom remained in any
one place for more than a day, and then only when the
people had been long neglected or when heresy or
paganism was rife. Miracles in the order of nature and of
grace accompanied his steps. (14:681)

The Catholic Encyclopedia Dictionary also notes: 'He is
said by some to have had the gift of tongues . . .' (1002).

COLETTE OF CORBI (d. 1447)
The following is recorded about Colette in *The Lives of the
Saints*:

In 1410, she founded a covenant at Besancon; in 1415,
she introduced a reform into the convent of the Cor-
deliers, at Dole, and in succession into nearly all the
convents in Lorraine, Champagne, and Picardy. In 1416,
she founded a house of her order at Poligny, at the foot of
the Jura, and another at Auxonne. 'I am dying of curiosity to see the wonderful Colette, who resuscitates the
dead,' wrote the Duchess of Bourbon, about this time.
For the fame of the miracles and labours of the carpen-
ter's daughter was in every mouth. (Baring-Gould, vol.
3, 1897:99–100)

The Reformation and the Modern Era, 1500–1900

MARTIN LUTHER (1483–1546)
In *Luther: Letters of Spiritual Counsel*, the following letter
of Martin Luther is recorded:

The tax collector in Torgau and the counsellor in Belgern
have written me to ask that I offer some good advice and
help for Mrs. John Korner's afflicted husband. I know of
no worldly help to give. If the physicians are at a loss to

find a remedy, you may be sure that it is not a case of ordinary melancholy. It must, rather, be an affliction that comes from the devil, and this must be counteracted by the power of Christ with the prayer of faith. This is what we do, and what we have been accustomed to do, for a cabinet maker here was similarly afflicted with madness and we cured him by prayer in Christ's name.

Accordingly you should proceed as follows: Go to him with the deacon and two or three good men. Confident that you, as pastor of the place, are clothed with the authority of the ministerial office, lay your hands upon him and say, 'Peace be with you, dear brother, from God our Father and from our Lord Jesus Christ.' Thereupon repeat the Creed and the Lord's Prayer over him in a clear voice, and close with these words: 'O God, almighty Father, who has told us through thy Son, "Verily, verily I say unto you, Whatsoever ye shall ask the Father in my name, he will give it you"; who has commanded and encouraged us to pray in his name, "Ask, and ye shall receive," and who in like manner hast said, "Call upon me in the day of trouble: I will deliver thee, and thou shalt glorify me"; we unworthy sinners, relying on these thy words and commands, pray for thy mercy with such faith as we can muster. Graciously deign to free this man from all evil, and put to nought the work that Satan has done in him, to the honour of thy name and the strengthening of the faith of believers; through the same Jesus Christ, thy Son, our Lord, who liveth and reigneth with thee, world without end. Amen.' Then, when you depart, lay your hands upon the man again and say, 'These signs shall follow them that believe; they shall lay hands on the sick, and they shall recover.' Do this three times, once on each of three successive days. (Tappert n.d.:52)

In *Luther's Works*, concerning prophecy he says, 'If you wish to prophesy, do it in such a way that it does not go beyond faith so that your prophesying can be in harmony with the peculiar quality of faith,' He goes on to write that 'one may prophesy new things but not things that go beyond the bounds of faith . . .' (Oswald n.d.:444–51).

IGNATIUS OF LOYOLA (1491–1556)

Ignatius was the founder of the Society of Jesus. He was wounded in the Spanish army in 1521. While recuperating he read the *Life of Christ* by Ludolph of Saxony. This inspired him to become a 'soldier' for Christ. He entered a monastery and spent nearly a year at ascetic practices. Here he composed the essence of his *Spiritual Exercises*. In them he writes the following about the Spirit:

> The Spirit of God breathes where he will; he does not ask our permission; he meets us on his own terms and distributes his charisms as He pleases. Therefore, we must always be awake and ready; we must be pliable so that he can use us in new enterprises. We cannot lay down the law to the Spirit of God! He is only present with his gifts where he knows that they are joined with the multiplicity of charisms in the one Church. All the gifts of this church stem from one source – God. What Paul says in the twelfth chapter of his First Epistle to the Corinthians is still true today! This should give us the strength to overcome every form of clerical jealousy, mutual suspicion, power-grabbing, and the refusal to let others – who have their own gifts of the Spirit – go on their own way. That is what the Spirit wants from us! He is not so narrow-minded as we sometimes are with our recipes! He can lead to himself in different ways, and He wants to direct the church through a multiplicity of functions, offices, and gifts. The church is not supposed to be a military academy in which everything is uniform, but she is supposed to be the body of Christ in which he, the one Spirit, exerts his power in all the members. Each one of these members proves that he really is a member of this body by letting the other members be. (Rahner 1962:254–5)

TERESA OF AVILA (1515–1582)

Teresa, a Carmelite reformer, mystic, and writer, was born in Spain and educated by Augustinian nuns. In her autobiography there are frequent accounts of the ecstasy she experienced from God. In it she writes, 'What I say about not ascending to God unless he raises one up is language of the Spirit. He who has had some experience will understand me, for I don't know how to describe this being raised up if it isn't understood through experience' (12:5). She refers to this kind of speech again when talking about prayer (16:1–2):

> I don't know any other terms for describing it or how to explain it. Nor does the soul then know what to do because it doesn't know whether to speak or to be silent, whether to laugh or to weep. This prayer is a glorious foolishness, a heavenly madness where the true wisdom is learned; and it is for the soul a most delightful way of enjoying. In fact five or even six years ago the Lord often gave me this prayer in abundance, and I didn't understand it; nor did I know how to speak of it.

VALENTINE GREATLAKES (d. 1638)

David Robertson writes in his article 'From Epidauros to Lourdes: A History of Healing by Faith' about an Irishman named Greatlakes:

> He was a Protestant in Catholic Ireland and fled to England in 1641 at the outbreak of the Irish Rebellion. For a time he served under Cromwell. In 1661, after a period of depression, he came to believe that God had given him, a mere commoner, the power to cure scrofula. When he began trying to cure the king's evil, his friends and acquaintances were astounded to find that he did indeed seem able to produce a regression in this disease. This stunning achievement led him to try his hand at other illnesses like epilepsy, paralysis, deafness, ulcers, and diverse nervous disorders, and he found that

his touch was efficacious in these cases as well. Soon word of his uncanny ability spread far and wide and he was besieged by multitudes of sick people. The crowds that came to him were so great that he could not accommodate all of them even if he worked from six in the morning until six at night. (Frazier 1973:187)

THE QUAKERS, OR THE SOCIETY OF FRIENDS (1640–present)

The Quakers' origins are traced back to English Puritanism in the 1640s. The first leader was George Fox, who preached a message of the New Age of the Spirit. They were opposed by both the Puritans and Anglicans. The typical Quaker meeting was characterised by the people waiting for the Spirit to speak through them and by the people 'quaking' as God moved among them. The following is an excerpt from Fox's *Journal*:

> In the year 1648, as I was sitting in a friend's house in Nottinghamshire (for by this time the power of God had opened the hearts of some to receive the word of life and reconciliation), I saw there was a great crack to go throughout the earth, and a great smoke to go as the crack went; and that after the crack there should be a great shaking: this was the earth in people's hearts, which was to be shaken before the seed of God was raised out of the earth. And it was so: for the Lord's power began to shake them and great meetings we begun to have, and mighty power and work of God there was amongst people, to the astonishment of both people and priests. (Fox 1901:23)

THE HUGUENOTS (Formally organised in 1559)

Huguenots was a nickname for the French Calvinists. Henry Baird writes in his book *The Huguenots* the following concerning some of the phenomena of this religious group:

Respecting the physical manifestations, there is little discrepancy between the accounts of friend and foe. The persons affected were men and women, the old and the young. Very many were children, boys and girls of nine or ten years of age. They were sprung from the people – their enemies said, from the dregs of the people – ignorant and uncultured; for the most part unable to read or write, and speaking in everyday life the *patois* of the province with which alone they were conversant. Such persons would suddenly fall backward, and, while extended at full length on the ground, undergo strange and apparently involuntary contortions; their chests would seem to heave, their stomachs to inflate. On coming gradually out of this condition, they appeared instantly to regain the power of speech. Beginning often in a voice interrupted by sobs, they soon poured forth a torrent of words – cries for mercy, calls to repentance, exhortations to the bystanders to cease frequenting the mass, denunciations of the church of Rome, prophecies of coming judgement. From the mouths of those that were little more than babes came texts of Scripture, and discourse in good and intelligible French, such as they never used in their conscious hours. When the trance ceased, they declared that they remembered nothing of what had occurred, or of what they had said. In rare cases they retained a general and vague impression, but nothing more. There was no appearance of deceit or collusion, and no indication that in uttering their predictions respecting coming events they had any thought of prudence, or doubt as to the truth of what they foretold. Brueys, their most inveterate opponent, is no less positive on this point than are the witnesses who are most favourable to them. 'These poor madmen', he said, 'believed that they were indeed inspired by the Holy Ghost. They prophesied without any (ulterior) design, without evil intent, and with so little reserve, that they always boldly marked the day, the place and persons of whom they spoke in their predictions.' (2:186–7)

THE JANSENISTS (c. 1731)

'The expectation of miracles and other supernatural signs had become almost an integral part of the Jansenist world-view by the end of the seventeenth century,' writes Robert Kreiser in his book *Miracles, Convulsions, and Ecclesiastical Politics in Early Eighteenth-Century Paris*. One such miracle that he records is the cure of Pascal's niece in March 1656. Marguerite had been suffering for a long time from a serious and disfiguring lachrymal fistula in the corner of her eye. She was healed when a holy thorn was simply touched to her eye. The miracle was supported by substantial medical evidence and made a profound impression on the public.

JOHN WESLEY (1703–91)

John Wesley was the founder of the Methodist Church. In his *Journal* he writes:

> Wed., Aug. 15, 1750 – By reflecting on an odd book which I had read in this journey, *The General Delusion of Christians with Regard to Prophecy*, I was fully convinced of what I had once suspected: (1) That the Montanists, in the second and third centuries, were real, scriptural Christians; and (2) That the grand reason why the miraculous gifts were so soon withdrawn, was not only that faith and holiness were wellnigh lost, but that dry, formal, orthodox men began even then to ridicule whatever gifts they had not themselves, and to decry them all as either madness or imposture.

Wesley wrote a letter to Thomas Church in June 1746 in which he states:

> Yet I do not know that God hath anyway precluded himself from thus exerting His sovereign power from working miracles in any kind or degree in any age to the end of the world. I do not recollect any scripture wherein we are taught that miracles were to be confined within the limits either of the apostolic or the Cyprianic age, or

of any period of time, longer or shorter, even till the restitution of all things. I have not observed, either in the Old Testament, or the New, any intimation at all of this kind. St. Paul says, indeed, once, concerning two of the miraculous gifts of the Spirit (so, I think, that test is usually understood), 'Whether there be prophecies, they shall fail; whether there be tongues, they shall cease.' But he does not say, either that these or any other miracles shall cease till faith and hope shall cease also, till they all be swallowed up in the vision of God, and love be all in all. (Telford n.d.:261)

Azusa Street (1906)

In 1905, Charles Parham moved his school from Topeka, Kansas, to Houston, Texas. There William J. Seymour, a black evangelist, joined the school. He embraced the 'teaching on tongues' but did not experience this in Houston. In 1906, Seymour was invited to speak in a small black Nazarene church in Los Angeles. On 1 April 1906, Seymour spoke in tongues. The small group soon outgrew the little house on Bonnie Brae and moved into an old livery stable at 312 Azusa Street.

Seymour was the central figure of the Azusa Street revival. The revival continued for three and a half years at Azusa Street. Services were held three times daily – morning, afternoon, and evening. Speaking in tongues was a central attraction, but healing of the sick was not far behind. Seymour was the pastor of the congregation, which was made up of both blacks and whites, until his death in 1929. Pilgrims to Azusa were common and came from all parts of the world, according to Frank Bartleman in *Azusa Street* (136).

APPENDIX B
SIGNS AND WONDERS IN THE TWENTIETH CENTURY

Signs and wonders are still occurring in this century, both apart from and under the immediate supervision of Western denominations. Indications are that churches grow most rapidly where Western Christians – and their anti-supernatural bent – have the least immediate influence.

The following are random case studies gathered by myself and others. I only recount examples that demonstrate the relationship between signs and wonders and church growth.

South Africa

In South Africa there is an Indian community of about eight hundred thousand that was solidly opposed to the Christian faith. Very few Indians became Christians. About twenty or twenty-five years ago, through a series of healing campaigns, two Pentecostal denominations began to grow among the Indians. One of those Pentecostal churches is now twenty-five thousand strong, the other fifteen thousand.[1]

REINHARD BONNKE
Bonnke is a German missionary ministering through an independent organisation called Christ for All Nations, mainly in the black homelands of South Africa. His first campaign was conducted in Gaberones, Botswana, with

the Apostolic Faith Mission (A.F.M.) which at that time had only forty members in the city. Nightly after preaching, Bonnke would be joined by Richard Ngidi to pray for the sick. After only six days they were attracting crowds of two thousand to an auditorium that seated eight hundred. Dramatic healings resulted and the meetings were moved to a stadium where they attracted a nightly audience of ten thousand people.

The next campaign was held in Sibasa, northern Transvaal. Within seven days after the occurrence of extraordinary miracles, the stadium was filled with a nightly audience of thirty thousand people despite heavy rains. In 1979, Bonnke held a campaign for the A.F.M. in Bloemfontein, South Africa. Hundreds were saved, healed, and baptised in water. After a campaign of twenty days they established a new church with a baptised membership of over six hundred people. Christ for All Nations has now built a tent that accommodates thirty-four thousand people and is using it regularly.[2]

ERLO STEGEN

Stegen is a German missionary working with the Zulus in Kwasizabantu in South Africa. The first twelve years of his ministry in their region were completely unsuccessful. At that point, totally frustrated, Stegen began a detailed study of the book of Acts with a group of black associates. They identified signs and wonders as being the key to the rapid growth of the early Church. Later they experienced the filling of the Holy Spirit. The details of that experience were described as being similar to the account in Acts 2.

Immediately after leaving the room where they had experienced the anointing of the Holy Spirit, Stegen and the group were met by a demon-possessed woman who said, 'Something just drove me to come here and ask you to pray for me.' They cast the demon out and the woman was delivered and set free. The woman returned to her village and caused a small revival. She preached the gospel, prayed for the sick, and hundreds gave their lives to the Lord.

From that point on people began streaming to Kwasiza-bantu. Those who were healed, saved, and filled with the Spirit went back to his or her own village and proclaimed the gospel there. This was the start of a large revival.[3]

Ivory Coast

PROPHET HARRIS

The prophet William Wade Harris, a Liberian of the Berbos tribe, grew up under the influence of Christianity. His uncle was a Methodist preacher in Liberia. At the age of twenty, Harris had a deep religious experience. However, his Christian ministry did not begin until he was sixty years old.

In 1913, 'Prophet Harris', as he was called, entered the Ivory Coast to embark on one of the greatest evangelistic tours ever recorded in African history. Rene Bureau in his unpublished dissertation 'The Prophet Harris' adds some insight on the way God called Prophet Harris to become a missionary. He reveals the testimony given to a Catholic priest in the Ivory Coast before Harris started his journey along the coast:

> I am a prophet of God. Four years ago I was awakened at night. I saw my guardian angel under my bed. He hit me three times on the forehead, saying, 'I am going to take your wife from you. She will die, but I will give you many people to help you. Before your wife dies, she will give you six shillings, that will be your fortune. You will never need anything, I will be with you always and reveal to you the mission of God.' That's why I have come. I am here to do God's mission.

William Harris then began his journey along the coastline of the Ivory Coast. He dressed in a white robe and turban, carried a Bible, a bamboo cross, and a gourd of water. He went everywhere proclaiming the message of salvation in

Christ. He never read from the Bible, because the people were illiterate, but he quoted from memory passages dealing with salvation. He taught songs and proclaimed that worship of fetishes and idols was wrong and God would punish people who practised such things. He challenged the people to burn their fetishes and follow God.

Harris would invite those wanting to follow God to come forward and kneel before the cross. They would come and place both hands on the bamboo cross, confessing their sins. Harris would then touch the tops of their heads with his Bible. The new converts would tremble, and Harris would expel demons.

In Jackville, Harris healed the chief's wife, who was dying. He said, 'Touch this cross, get up, and walk.' She did, and the entire village was converted.

He organised groups of believers and advised them to construct chapels. He placed a pastor in charge of each and had each group select twelve apostles to direct the church. Some converts were sent to the interior tribes to bring them the message of salvation. Harris told these newly formed congregations that missionaries would come to explain the Bible.

After two years of ministry in the Ivory Coast, Harris was arrested by the French authorities and sent back to Liberia. The French feared this new religious movement and attempted to stop it.[4]

JACQUES GIRAUD

The church in the Ivory Coast was typical of the church in many countries of Asia, Africa, and Latin America. The Ivory Coast has about four million people, with the Roman Catholic Church claiming about thirty thousand. The Methodist Church dates from 1924 and has sixty thousand. Seven small Protestant denominations, with a total baptised membership of about eleven thousand, have arisen because of the faithful work of missionaries. Their growth rate is 70 percent per decade. (About a hundred and fifty dedicated missionaries from America, Switzerland and

France are helping these churches and are doing a multitude of good deeds.)

Pastor Jacques Giraud, a French missionary to the West Indies, arrived in the Ivory Coast in March 1973 to dedicate an Assemblies of God church building in Abidjan. As the meetings progressed, people began to be healed. The crowds grew and the meetings were moved to the stadium. Truckloads of people came from all parts of the Ivory Coast. The papers and radio stations reported the events. Leading government officials and their wives flocked to the stadium.

Pastor Giraud would tell about one of Christ's miracles and preach for an hour on God's almighty power to heal. Then he would say, 'I don't heal. God heals, I ask him to release his power. Put your hand where it hurts and join me in prayer.' He would pour out his heart in believing prayer to God for healing. After a half hour of prayer he would invite those God had healed to come to the front. Crutches were thrown away. Bent and arthritic persons stood erect. Blind men walked forward seeing. Scores and sometimes hundreds came. God had given them at least a measure of healing. (Thousands were also not healed.)

Although he was a minister of the Assemblies of God denomination, it was his practice to direct converts to the local churches and missions for shepherding. At Toumoudi he had the Christian and Missionary Alliance missionaries and ministers on the platform with him. He said to the people, 'When you place your faith in Jesus Christ, call these men to baptise you and shepherd you.'

Reverend Fred Pilding, a missionary of the Christian and Missionary Alliance working in the Ivory Coast, fills in some details in the *Alliance Witness*, 26 September 1973:

The crusade began in Bouake on June 18th and continued for three weeks. Morning attendance averaged about 4,000. From 6,000 to 15,000 turned out in the evenings with a high of 25,000 one Sunday. The sick were seated on the grass on the playing field, and all the others occupied the grandstands. As the evangelist presented Jesus Christ, the same yesterday, today, and forever, people became aware of his continuing power today, through a healing receptive place. It became easier for them to trust him as Saviour.

A hunchback came to the meeting, grovelling in the dirt, under the influence of demons. The demons were exorcised in the name of Jesus and he was instantly healed. The next day he attended the meetings nicely dressed, perfectly calm, and gave his testimony.

Whenever those who were healed testified, witnesses were asked to verify each healing. Pastor Giraud again and again cited Mark 16:15–18 as every believer's commission and emphasised that in Christ's name they were to cast out devils and lay hands on the sick and they shall recover. He refuted vigorously the title of healer. His ministry, he said, was to inspire faith in the gospel. 'It is in the name of Jesus that people are healed.'

After the Toumoudi meeting, groups of converts from 81 villages around Toumoudi sought out the Alliance missionaries and ministers, begging them to come and make them Christians. After the Bouake meeting, responses were received from over 100 villages. A hundred and forty cards were filled out from one small town alone.

From one village near Bouake ten cards had been received. The missionary went to visit this village. Seeing him, one of the men who had been healed rushed off to get some of the pagan village elders. While waiting, the missionary said to the children, 'Do you know Pastor Giraud's song?' Immediately they broke into joyful singing, 'Up, up with Jesus, down, down with Satan, Alleluia!' People came pouring out and the missionary preached and then asked, 'How many will follow God and leave their old ways?' More than half immediately said, 'We will.' In another village the Chief said, 'Fetish is dead, we shall all become Christians.'

The pastors and missionaries were faced with great

opportunities. The challenge was to take advantage of this enthusiasm, which could dissipate rapidly, and channel these people into ongoing responsible churches of Christians who know the Lord, obey his word. Nothing like this had happened in their experience on the Ivory Coast, and they were naturally fearful, lest the excitement prove transient as it very well might.[5]

Argentina

TOMMY HICKS

In 1952, God spoke to American evangelist Tommy Hicks through a vision, telling him to go to South America and preach the gospel. In 1954, while on his way to Buenos Aires, the name Peron flashed into Hicks' mind. He knew nobody by that name. Near the flight's destination he asked the flight attendant whether she knew anybody by that name. She replied, 'Yes, Mr Peron is the president of Argentina.' Hicks sought an appointment with Mr Peron but ran into difficulties. Then an extraordinary event took place at the president's office. While seeking an interview, Hicks encountered Mr Peron's secretary, who had a bad leg. Hicks prayed for him and he was instantly healed. This resulted in Hicks being introduced to General Peron.

Peron received Hicks warmly and instructed his assistant to give Hicks whatever he asked for. On Hicks' request, a large stadium was made available to him as well as free access to the government-controlled radio and press. The campaign lasted for fifty-two days. Hicks preached the gospel of the saving power of Jesus, emphasising divine healing. Over two million people attended the meetings. Some two hundred thousand people attended the campaign on the final night. Although almost all the local churches grew as a result of the campaign, the Assemblies of God gained the most. Their growth, from 174 in 1951 to nearly two thousand members in 1956, reflects the tremendous impact of Hicks' campaign.[6]

India

Suba Rao was the headmaster of a government school in India, a member of one of the middle castes and a wealthy man. He hated missionaries and laughed at baptism. He thought of the church as an assembly of the low castes (which in India it was).

One of his near neighbours and close friends fell sick. He was sick for two years and was gradually wasting away. He went to many doctors, to no avail. One night, while Suba Rao was asleep, the Lord Jesus appeared to him and said, 'If you will go and lay your hand on that man's head and pray in my name, I will heal him.' Suba Rao woke up and laughed; he thought it was a funny dream and went back to sleep.

The next night the Lord Jesus stood by his side and said, 'If you go and lay your hand on that man's head and pray for him to be healed, I will heal him.' Suba Rao woke up. He didn't laugh this time, and he didn't go back to sleep; but he didn't lay his hands on the sick man either. He thought, 'That's impossible!' The third night the Lord Jesus appeared to him again. This time he got up at once and went to his neighbour. He laid his hand on the man's head, prayed for him, and in the morning the man said, 'I feel much better. Do it again.' The man was healed.

Suba Rao threw out his idols. He started to read the Bible. He started a Bible study class among his neighbours. Still today he ridicules baptism. He has still not joined any church, but he proclaims himself a follower of the Lord Jesus. The healing of people in Jesus' name has become his chief occupation. Joining the church, which in India is composed largely of the lowest castes of Indian society is, he thinks, an impossible step for him. Still, the Lord Jesus heals men through Suba Rao.[7]

THE NISHI TRIBALS
The Nishi Tribals in Sulansini Division in India are now

receptive to the miraculous. It all started when a high government official's youngest son fell terminally ill:

> A Hindu pharmacist, recognising that the child was beyond medical help, advised that the father 'Try the Christian God, Jesus Christ. I have once heard that he had raised a man called Lazarus, who had already been dead for three days!' As the father approached his house, he heard crying and wailing, and he knew that his son must have died. He went into the house, discovered that it was so, but then went into the son's room, placed his hand on the chest of his dead son and prayed. 'Jesus, I do not know who you are, but I have just heard that you raised Lazarus from the dead after three days. My son has died only a few hours ago, and if you raise him up, I promise you, even though I do not know who you are, my family and I will worship you.' Immediately the eyes of the child began to flicker again and he was restored to life. The impact of the miracle was tremendous. The people cried, 'Jesus, who are you? What love you have for us!' Within the next couple of weeks, hundreds gave their lives to Jesus.[8]

China

David Wang is the general director of Asian Outreach. He visits mainland China quite often and has regular contact with the believers there. His reports of what the Lord is doing in China are very exciting.

For example, he tells us that near Foochon, there is a place called Christian Mountain. The community of Christian Mountain consists of between thirty and fifty thousand people, of whom 90 percent are Christians. The growth of this Christian community can be related directly to the deliverance of a girl possessed by demons in 1969–70.

Indonesia

The well-known German theologian Kurt Koch did some excellent research on what is now called the 'revival in Indonesia'. Timor is one of the islands at the eastern extremity of Indonesia. Out of a population of one million, some four hundred and fifty thousand people belong to the former Dutch Reformed Church. According to Koch, by the early 1960s the spiritual state of the churches was almost catastrophic. Timor had never been evangelised; only 'Christianised'. In 1964, in a vision, God instructed a man named Jephtah (a teacher on the island of Rote) to travel to Timor and hold a healing campaign there. From the start of the campaign God confirmed Jephtah's calling with a mighty ministry of signs and wonders. Following the close of the campaign, a further week of healing was held in Sol. According to various reports, which were later confirmed, several thousand people were healed. All of this was the start of what developed into a mighty revival, with thousands being saved. In one area an evangelistic team won more than nine thousand people for Christ in just two weeks.

Canada

RED SUCKER LAKE, MANITOBA, 1951

A young couple, new missionaries, were spending their first winter of marriage in an isolated Cree Indian village near Red Sucker Lake. It was towards springtime, and lakes and rivers were clogged with ice, making float flying (landing planes on lakes) impossible. There was neither telephone nor radio communication to the outside.

The missionaries were in the initial stages of learning the Indian language. The small child of a prominent native became very seriously ill. There were no medical facilities in the village and the workers had no medical training. As the child's state worsened, friends suggested that perhaps one of the new missionaries would pray for the child. The child's father refused, saying, 'He's a false teacher, how could he do any good?' The days passed and the child's condition became critical, until it was clear to all he was dying. The neighbours said, 'Well, it can't hurt now to let him pray for him. The child's dying anyway.' The father reluctantly yielded. The missionary came to the tent, prayed briefly for the child to get well, then left. The next day the child had completely recovered. Today, the grown child is living a normal life, happily married. Eventually the father was converted, went to Bible school, and became the pastor of the Indian church in the village.[9]

APPENDIX C
TURNING THE EVANGELICAL KEY

The face of evangelicalism is changing, and it is changing quickly. According to David B. Barrett, in 1990 there were 405 million Pentecostals and charismatics worldwide; by the year 2000 Barrett estimates there will be 619 million! Fundamentalists and conservative evangelicals, who are noncharismatic, can no longer afford to ignore the first two waves of the Holy Spirit in this century. They are surrounded.[1]

One of these two groups, the fundamentalists, have insulated themselves from Pentecostals and charismatics. Most fundamentalists (though not all) stand outside the first two great waves of the Holy Spirit, holding on to fifty-year-old criticisms of Pentecostal excesses. As the movement of the Holy Spirit grows around them, I believe many of them could become more vocal in their opposition to Pentecostals and charismatics, while some will be softened and even open their hearts to the work of the Spirit.

The second group, the conservative evangelicals, is the object of a new wave, the Third Wave, of the Holy Spirit's work in this century. C. Peter Wagner coined the term 'Third Wave'. Here is what he said about it in the January 1986 issue of *Christian Life* magazine:

> The term 'Third Wave' has been with us for about three years. It seems to have caught on to a considerable degree. People now know we are not referring to Alvin Toffler's book of the same name, but to the third wave of the power of the Holy Spirit in the twentieth century.

. . . The Third Wave began around 1980 with the opening of an increasing number of traditional evangelical churches and institutions to the supernatural working of the Holy Spirit, even though they were not, nor did they wish to become, either Pentecostal or charismatic.

. . . One of the characteristics of the Third Wave is the absence of divisiveness. Many churches which do not have Pentecostal or charismatic backgrounds are beginning to pray for the sick and witness God's healing power while avoiding what some have considered (rightly and wrongly) the excesses of the past.

Dr Wagner's last point, about the absence of divisiveness, is what excites me most about the Third Wave. Donald G. Bloesch writes,

The only genuine spiritual way to true . . . unity [among Christians] is a return to the message and teachings of Scripture with the aid of the tradition of the whole church. *Yet this return will involve not only an acceptance of right doctrine but also a renewal of personal faith . . . The conversion that we call for is a spiritual as well as an intellectual one.*[2]

True unity among Christians will come only when issues that divide them are addressed. In the remainder of this Appendix I will address the concerns of many conservative evangelicals about the ministry of the Holy Spirit today.

*   *   *

Theology is *very* important in one way or another for conservative evangelicals. At one point, however, their theology is an obstacle to their understanding signs and wonders. Part of the theological heritage of conservative evangelicals denies that the gifts function today. So a major issue that must be addressed so as to further conservative evangelical and charismatic unity is theological: the cessation theory of the charismatic gifts.

There seem to be two fundamental ways of trying to prove biblically that the miraculous gifts have ceased and are not for today. The first argument says *miraculous gifts were integral to the office of an apostle, and they ceased when the apostolic office or gift ceased at the end of the first century*. Further, the primary purpose of supernatural gifts was to authenticate the apostolic office or the apostolic message. In other words, the miraculous gifts were necessary to establish the Church, but not to maintain it. (Passages like Ephesians 2:20, 1 Corinthians 4:9 and 15:8, and Hebrews 2:3–4 are interpreted as meaning the office of apostleship was limited to the first century.) The second primary argument for the cessation of miraculous gifts asserts that *miracles are connected with canonical revelation. When the New Testament was completed, miraculous gifts ceased*.

There is, however, not much biblical evidence for either of these positions. B. B. Warfield, a late nineteenth- and early twentieth-century theologian whose book *Counterfeit Miracles*[3] remains influential today, argues that only apostles and those who had hands laid on by the apostles received supernatural gifts. At best, though, his is an argument from silence. Scripture presents the lives of special people as examples to copy. But when many modern Christians read about the apostles, Stephen, Philip, Agabus, and others in the book of Acts, they assume that their divine guidance and miracles are not to be copied or even hoped for today. Yet this assumption does not have clear scriptural support.

Are there really only a few in the New Testament who experienced the miraculous gifts? What about the Seventy-two in Luke 10:17? In the book of Acts there were the one hundred and twenty (1:15), Cornelius and the Gentiles (10:44–6), Ananias (9:10–18), the prophet Agabus (11:28; 21:10–11), the individuals named in 13:1, the prophets Judas and Silas (15:32), and Philip's four virgin daughters (21:9). There is no evidence that the apostles laid hands on any of them in order that they should receive miraculous gifts. In fact, it was Ananias, a non-apostle, who laid hands on Paul and saw him filled with the Holy Spirit!

The epistles too are full of examples of non-apostles experiencing supernatural gifts. Paul tells the Corinthians that none of the gifts are missing among them (1 Cor. 1:7), and Peter says that 'each one' has received a spiritual gift (1 Pet. 4:10). Prophecy was in use in Rome (Rom. 12:6), Thessalonica (1 Thess. 5:20), and Ephesus (Eph. 4:11). And the way Paul mentions miracles in the letter to the Galatians suggests that miracles were common among them (Gal. 3:5). After looking at the biblical evidence I conclude that miraculous gifts were not confined to apostles and those they laid their hands on.

Further, there is no biblical evidence that the sole purpose of signs and wonders was to authenticate the apostles' ministry. If so, why did so many non-apostles experience them?

Moreover, the New Testament does ascribe other important functions to signs and wonders. First, they authenticate Jesus' relationship with his heavenly Father – that he is the Messiah and the Son of God (Matt. 11:1–6; 14:25–32). In other words, they authenticate the person and mission of Jesus. Second, by attesting to the message of the gospel, they help lead people to repentance and belief in Jesus, as seen in the preaching ministry of the apostles (Rom. 15:18–19; Acts 13:11) and in their written ministry (John 20:30–1). In addition to what they authenticate, the gifts of the Spirit are given to the *whole church*, according to Paul, 'for the common good' (1 Cor. 12:7), for the edification of the whole body (also see 1 Cor. 14:3).

If Jesus and the message concerning Jesus required authentication in the first century, why isn't it required today? Why were signs and wonders required even *after* his resurrection and ascension, as recorded in the book of Acts? Why is there no biblical text that indicates God has done away with the authenticating function of the miraculous, or that the Church is no longer in need of miraculous authentication for the message of the gospel? I conclude that miraculous authentication is as valid today as it was in the first century.

*   *   *

A more popular cessation theory is based on an interpretation of 1 Corinthians 13:10: '. . . but when *perfection* comes, the imperfect disappears'. Many conservative evangelicals teach that 'perfection' here refers to the completed canon of Scripture (the New Testament), recognised at the Council of Carthage in 397; and that 'the imperfect' refers to the charismatic gifts, which have now 'disappeared' or ceased.

Referring to the supernatural gifts, one popular author writes,

> These [miracles, healing, tongues, and interpretation of tongues] were certain enablements given to certain believers for the purpose of authenticating or confirming God's word when it was proclaimed in the early church before the scriptures were penned. These sign gifts were temporary . . . Once the Word of God was inscriptured, the sign gifts were no longer needed and they ceased.[4]

The argument for equating 'perfection' with the closing of the New Testament canon has two parts. First, the word 'perfection' is a neuter noun, and must, they imply, refer to a thing, not a person. Since Scripture is a thing and is neuter in gender, it follows that the Bible is the 'perfect' thing to which Paul is referring. Second, this interpretation, they assert, fits well with verses 8, 9, 11 and 12 of the same passage in 1 Corinthians 13: '. . . where there are tongues, they will be stilled . . . For we know in part . . . When I was a child, I talked like a child . . . Now I know in part; then I shall know fully, even as I am fully known.' In this line of reasoning, tongues are childish, while Scripture is mature.

There are several weaknesses with this interpretation, not the least of which is that a major doctrine is being built on a fairly unclear passage. Where else in Scripture is there a hint of this teaching?

Beyond this, while 'perfection' is a neuter noun, in Greek there is no warrant for limiting its reference to another neuter noun. A neuter noun or pronoun can be used to describe masculine or feminine things or persons. One example is the Greek word translated 'child' (*teknon*). Though neuter in gender, this noun may describe a little girl or boy. The point is that in Greek – much like German – gender is grammatical, not sexual.

Perhaps a bigger problem is that their interpretation calls for the leaving of the immediate context of 1 Corinthians 13 to determine the identity of 'perfection'. They arbitrarily jump to 2 Timothy 3:15–16. A better interpretation of 'perfection' is that it refers to the *situation* or *state of affairs* that will occur when Christ returns, the 'perfect state' which Paul describes in 1 Corinthians 13:12: 'Now we see but a poor reflection as in a mirror; then we shall see face to face. Now I know in part; then I shall know fully, even as I am fully known.' The Greek neuter case would be naturally used to refer to this future situation.[5]

*　　*　　*

It would be a mistake to think theology is the only obstacle to conservative evangelical and charismatic unity. In fact, I have discovered that attempts to unify around theology are unsatisfying. Fear, for example, is another barrier. In particular there is the fear that the authority of Scripture will be undermined by gifts like prophecy and tongues, that subjective experience will replace objective truth as the plumb-line of Christianity.

There is also a cultural barrier. Conservative evangelicals have in recent years increased their social, economic and educational status, making it harder for them to relate to Pentecostals.[6] Pentecostals too have been moving up the social scale, though not as rapidly as conservative evangelicals. On the other hand, many conservative evangelicals have been favourably affected by the charismatic renewal (by people of a social standing closer to theirs), even when, due to theological reservations, they have not experienced the gifts.

Another wave of the Holy Spirit, one affecting conservative evangelicals, has come with different models of how the charismatic gifts should function, such as in power evangelism. Just as Pentecostalism and the charismatic renewal have produced different results as they have affected different groups of people, this move of renewal has a different flavour, with a particular emphasis on personal evangelism. C. Peter Wagner reflects this thinking when replying to a question about whether he considers himself a charismatic or Pentecostal:

> I see myself as neither a charismatic nor a Pentecostal. I belong to Lake Avenue Congregational Church. I'm a Congregationalist. My church is not a charismatic church, although some of our members are charismatic.
>
> However, our church is more and more open to the same way that the Holy Spirit does work among charismatics. For example, our pastor gives an invitation after every service for people who need physical healing and inner healing to come forward and go to the prayer room and be anointed with oil and prayed for, and we have teams of people who know how to pray for the sick.
>
> We like to think that we are doing it in a Congregational way; we're not doing it in a charismatic way. But we're getting the same results.[7]

The Third Wave emphasises the universal priesthood of all Christians. The only requirements to ride that wave are a hunger for God and a humility to receive him on his terms. Your power encounter is only as far away as this prayer: 'Holy Spirit, I open my heart, my innermost being to you. I turn from my sin and self-sufficiency and ask that you fill me with your love, power and gifts. Come, Holy Spirit.'

NOTES

Chapter 2

1. The Hebrew understanding of time was different from that of the Greeks. For the Hebrews, God's purpose moves to a consummation (this is called a linear view of time). By contrast, the cyclical view of time was common in the ancient world, a view in which events just go on or return to the point whence they began, with no sense of purpose or direction. The New Testament Greek words that we translate eternity (*eis ton aiona*, usually translated 'for ever') literally mean 'for ages' (see also Mark 3:29; Luke 1:33, 55; Gal. 1:5; 1 Pet. 4:11; Rev. 1:18). The Hebrew concept of time emphasised the times appointed by God to fulfil his purposes on earth. Finally, the Hebrews divided history into two stages. The first, this age, is evil; the second, the age to come, is good.
2. George Ladd, *A Theology of the New Testament* (Guildford: Lutterworth Press, 1974), 48.
3. Ibid., 69.

Chapter 3

1. Much of this chapter is based on material gleaned from the writings of George Ladd and James Kallas. For those readers interested in further reading on the kingdom of God, I recommend Ladd's *A Theology of the New Testament* and Kallas' *The Real Satan* (Minneapolis, MN: Augsburg, 1975). For a view similar to Ladd's, Catholic readers may refer to Rudolf Schnackenburg's *The Moral Teaching of the New Testa-*

ment (New York: Seabury, 1965), especially chapter 1. Schnackenburg fits Jesus' moral demands 'principally (though not exclusively) within the framework of his gospel of the reign of God' (13).

2. I do not imply that Satan is equal in power to Christ. Any authority that Satan has is derived from God. For a time, God has permitted Satan to afflict the world so Christ's mercy and judgement can be demonstrated in the creation, especially in his work on the cross.

3. The Greek word used in the New Testament for 'church', *ekklesia*, was also used in the Greek translation of the Old Testament (the Septuagint). It literally means 'the called out ones', again indicating that the New Testament Church stands in direct continuity with the Old Testament people of God.

4. For greater depth on the relationship between the kingdom and the Church, see Ladd, *A Theology of the New Testament*, 111–19.

Chapter 4

1. Jesus came into the world to save men and women from Satan, to forgive and regenerate us, to offer eternal life to all who believe in him. The focus of this book is signs and wonders for the purpose of overcoming Satan's kingdom and as an avenue for leading many to Christ. By focusing on signs and wonders I imply neither that they are the totality of our salvation, nor that the analogy of the Church as an army is the only way to understand it. We are also called a family, a refuge, a people, a nation, and so on, each connoting different aspects of God's purpose in salvation.

Chapter 5

1. Kallas, *The Real Satan*, 60.
2. George Ladd, *The Presence of the Future* (Grand Rapids, MI: Eerdmans, 1974), 160–1.
3. Ibid., 162.

Chapter 6

1. Many questions about demonisation are raised in this illustration and throughout the chapter. For example, what is the relationship between personality disorders and demon possession? How can one tell the difference between the two? Questions like these are important but, I regret, not the focus of this book. My purpose in raising these questions here is so that readers may understand that I am dealing with only one aspect of a complex subject. See John Wimber and Kevin Springer, *Power Healing* (London: Hodder & Stoughton, 1986), 97–125.
2. Alan R. Tippett, *People Movements in Southern Polynesia* (Chicago: Moody Press, 1971).
3. C. Peter Wagner, 'Special Kinds of Church Growth' (Class notes, Fuller Theological Seminary, 1984), 14.
4. This testimony is drawn from an interview with Pradip Sudra in January 1991, conducted at Fuller Theological Seminary, Pasadena, CA.

Chapter 7

1. Oscar Cullmann, *Christ and Time* (Philadelphia: Westminster Press, 1964), 64.
2. Karl Ludwig Schmidt, '*Ethnos* in the NT', G. Kittel (ed.), *Theological Dictionary of the New Testament*, vol. 2 (Grand Rapids, MI: Eerdmans, 1964), 369.

Chapter 8

1. See Appendices A and B, where I give illustrations of power encounters in the history of the Church.
2. John Wesley, *The Works of John Wesley*, 3rd ed. (Peabody, MA: Hendrickson Publishers, 1984), vol. 1, 170.
3. Here is an example of the way people have responded to this kind of experience. Kevin Springer, after speaking at Emmaus Fellowship, a church in Ann Arbor, Michi-

gan, in November 1984, several months later received this letter from Martha Slauter, a woman he prayed for that day:

I wanted to share with you my experiences since you prayed over me at Emmaus. I had asked you to pray for a spirit of bitterness and resentment to leave. You did that and then stopped and said you felt there was something more – and then said you thought I had a very hard time trusting people. You prayed over me for an anointing of God's own trust for people. I want to share with you that even after church I just *felt* trusting and felt the Lord doing something different in my relationships with the sisters. I felt the Lord ministering the love he has for me through them. When we came home from church and were discussing everything, I shared with Gary [her husband] that I wanted to go and talk with Dr Dave King [a Christian counsellor]. That was significant in itself in that I never would have been open to that at all before. I've been under bondage to mistrust and letting circumstances get the best of me, to the point of sinking into self-pity and letting depression set in. The Lord showed me that he wanted to get these things taken care of once and for all, that he had victory for me and wanted to heal all these areas in me to enable me to go on with him, free of all encumbrances. Dr King has been a blessing to both of us and has helped us uncover a lot of garbage. It has been like turning a light on – the searching light of God's Spirit. The Lord has really used the counseling to reveal some bad patterns in relating with people that I had developed just from the way I had been raised and through subsequent relationships before and after I came to the Lord. It has been incredible! The amazing thing to me is just how gentle and loving and merciful God's 'spiritual surgery' is! The Lord also used two times I was prayed over and literally fell to the floor to do a lot of his work. I have never felt condemned by God as he points out all these problem areas, only tremendously reassured of his love and pleasure in me. I have previously had a problem in feeling condemned by everything.

Chapter 9

1. Anonymous, 'Where the Spirit of the Lord Is', *New Covenant*, October 1978, 15–16.
2. Werner Foerster, '*Exousia*', *Theological Dictionary of the New Testament*, vol. 2, 568.

Chapter 11

1. I do not mean to imply that power evangelism is the only kind of evangelism practised in the New Testament. Nor do I imply that power evangelism has been the most common type practised by Christians throughout church history. For example, evangelicals assert that the proclamation of the gospel message has intrinsic spiritual power, an assertion I would not deny. But my point remains: power evangelism was one of the normal kinds of evangelism in the early Church and has surfaced throughout the history of the Church with remarkable results.
2. C. Peter Wagner, 'A Third Wave?' *Pastoral Renewal*, July–August 1983, 1–5.
3. *Christianity Today*, 11 March 1991, 72.
4. This statistic, an estimate, comes from many conversations with leading missiologists at Fuller Theological Seminary's School of World Mission. Cf. Craig Hanscome, 'Predicting Missionary Dropout', *Evangelical Missions Quarterly* (1979), 152–5.
5. *National & International Religion Report*, 11 March 1991, 2.

Chapter 12

1. The following summarises these instances:

Works of Power	Preaching	Church Growth
Pentecost (2:4)	Peter (2:14)	3,000 added (2:41)
Cripple healed (3:1)	Peter (3:12)	5,000 believed (4:4)
Miraculous signs (8:6)	Philip (8:6)	Men and women believe (8:12)
Philip appears (8:26)	Philip teaches (8:35)	Eunuch baptised (8:38)
Angel appears, vision (10:3, 12, 44)	Peter (10:34)	Gentiles baptised; Spirit falls (10:47)
Lord's hand with them (11:20–1)	Men from Cyprus (11:20)	Many believe (11:21)
Evidence of God's grace (11:23–4)	Barnabas (11:23)	Great number believe (11:24b)
Holy Spirit falls (13:1–3)	Barnabas, Saul (13:1)	Churches in Asia, Europe
Miraculous signs and wonders (14:1–7)	Paul and Barnabas (14:3)	People divided (14:4, 21, 22)
Cripple healed (14:8–18)	Paul and Barnabas (14:15)	Disciples gather (14:21)
Cast out demon (16:16)	Paul and Silas (16:14)	Believers gather (16:40)
Earthquake, prison-doors open (16:25–6)	Paul and Silas (16:31–2)	Jailer and household saved (16:34)
God's power (18:1; cf. 1 Cor. 2:1, 4, 5)	Paul (18:5)	Many believed (18:8)
Extraordinary miracles (19:11–12)	Paul (19:10)	Churches in Asia

Chapter 13

1. D. Martyn Lloyd-Jones, *Joy Unspeakable* (Eastbourne: Kingsway, 1984), 75.

Chapter 15

1. Viggo Sogaard, M.A. project, 'Commissioned to Communicate: Cassettes in the Context of a Total Christian Communication Program', Wheaton Graduate School, Wheaton, Illinois, 1973. Also, cf. Viggo Sogaard, *Everything You Need to Know for a Cassette Ministry* (Minneapolis, MN: Bethany Publishing Company, 1975).
2. James Engel and Wilbert Norton, *What's Gone Wrong with the Harvest?* (Grand Rapids, MI: Zondervan, 1975), 45.

Chapter 17

1. This material is drawn from interviews with Jerry Brown, an Assemblies of God missionary from Equador and a close friend of Dr Flores. The interviews were conducted at Fuller Theological Seminary, Pasadena, CA, in February 1991.

Chapter 18

1. James Sire, *The Universe Next Door* (Leicester: Inter-Varsity Press, 1976), 17.
2. Charles Kraft, *Christianity and Culture* (Maryknoll, NY: Orbis Books, 1979), 53.
3. Charles H. Kraft, *Christianity with Power* (Ann Arbor MI: Vine, 1989), 20.

Chapter 19

1. John Maroom, Jr., 'The Fire Down South', *Forbes*, 15 October 1990, 56.

2. Ibid., 57.
3. Ibid., 64.
4. Paul Hiebert, 'The Flaw of the Excluded Middle', *Missiology*, 10.1 (1982), 35–47.

Chapter 20

1. Harry Blamires, *The Christian Mind* (London: SPCK, 1963), 44.
2. Lesslie Newbigin, *Foolishness to the Greeks* (London: SPCK, 1986), 14.

Chapter 21

1. See John Wimber and Kevin Springer, *Power Healing* (London: Hodder & Stoughton, 1986), chapter 7.
2. Blamires, *The Christian Mind*, 44.
3. Ibid., 67.
4. Ibid., 86.
5. Ibid., 106.
6. Kraft, *Christianity with Power*, 104, 108–14.

Chapter 22

1. Kraft, *Christianity and Culture*, 60. Dr Kraft shows how this assumption/conclusion process works. Here are some cultural features and the assumptions and conclusions that are reached using each one:

Cultural Feature	Assumption	Conclusion
Clothing	1. Immodest to go naked (USA)	1. Must wear clothes even to bed.

	2. One covers one's body if hiding something (Gava people, Nigeria)	2. Go naked to prove yourself.
	3. For ornamentation only (Higi people, Nigeria)	3. Wear on occasion only. Rearrange or change in public.
Buying	1. Impersonal, economic transaction (USA)	1. Fixed prices. No interest in seller as person. Get it over quickly.
	2. Social, person-to-person affair (Africa, Asia, Latin America)	2. Dicker over price. Establish personal relationship. Take time.
Youthfulness	1. Desirable (USA)	1. Look young, act young. Use cosmetics.
	2. Tolerated; something to be overcome (Africa)	2. Prove yourself mature. Don't act young.
Age	1. Undesirable (USA)	1. Dreaded. Old people unwanted.
	2. Desirable (Africa)	2. Old people revered.
Education	1. Primarily formal, outside home, teacher-centered (USA)	1. Formal schools. Hired specialists.

2. Primarily informal, in the home, learner-centered, traditional (Africa)	2. Learn by doing. Discipleship. Proverbs and folktales.

2. Kraft, *Christianity with Power*, 122.

Chapter 23

1. Herman Ridderbos, *The Coming of the Kingdom* (Philadelphia: Presbyterian and Reformed, 1962), xi.
2. C. Peter Wagner, *Church Growth and the Whole Gospel* (New York: Harper & Row, 1981). See also Luke 4:18–19; 7:21–2; Mark 16:17–18. (Note that I have added calming storms and feeding thousands.)
3. Ibid.
4. Cf. Colin Brown (ed.), *New International Dictionary of New Testament Theology*, vol. 2 (Exeter: Paternoster Press, 1976), 631.
5. Rene Laurentin, *Miracles in El Paso* (Ann Arbor, MI: Servant, 1982).

Chapter 24

1. *Evangelicals and Social Concern, An Evangelical Commitment*, Grand Rapids Report, No. 21, 1982, 9–11, 30–2.
2. James Dunn, *Jesus and the Spirit* (London: SCM Press, 1975), 48–9.

Chapter 25

1. John Wilkinson, *Health and Healing* (New York: Columbia University Press, 1980). Wilkinson's analysis demonstrates that of all the verses in the Gospels, those related to healing are in the following proportions:

Matthew, 9 percent; Mark, 20 percent; Luke, 12 percent; John, 13 percent.

2. Edward Langton, *Essentials of Demonology: A Study of
Jewish and Christian Doctrine, Its Origin and Development* (London: Epworth Press, 1949), 173.

Chapter 27

1. Jairus' daughter: Matthew 9:18–26; Mark 5:21–43;
Luke 8:40–56. Lazarus: John 11:1–12:19. The widow's
son: Luke 7:11–17. The 'many holy people': Matthew
27:52–3. (Old Testament cases include: the widow of
Zarephath's son, 1 Kings 17:17–24; the Shunammite
woman's son, 2 Kings 4:18–37; Elisha's bones, 2 Kings
13:14–21. Other New Testament cases include: Peter
raising Dorcas, Acts 9:36–42; Paul raising Eutychus,
Acts 20:7–12.)

Chapter 28

1. Robert K. Johnston (ed.), *The Use of the Bible in
Theology – Evangelical Options* (Atlanta, GA: John
Knox Press, 1985).

Chapter 31

1. Speaking gifts:

Example	Result
Tongues (Acts 10:44, 46)	Baptised believers (10:47–8)
Prophecy (13:1)	
Tongues/Prophecy (19:1–7)	Conversion of John the Baptist's disciples (19:5–7)

2. Visions:

Example	Result
Paul, Macedonia (Acts 16:9)	European churches
Paul (18:9)	Church at Corinth

3. Miracles:

Example	*Result*
Ananias/Sapphira (5:1–11)	Fear (5:11,13)
Spirit caught up Philip (8:39)	
Paul blinded (9:1–9a)	
Elymas blinded (13:4–12)	Sergius Paulus believed (13:12)
Paul stoned/raised (14:19–20)	Disciples (14:21)

4. Healings:

Example:	*Result*
Lame man (3:7–8)	Numbers grew to five thousand (4:4)
Sick and those tormented by evil (5:16)	More healed (5:16)
Paul's blindness healed (9:17–19)	
Lame man in Lystra (14:10)	Disciples (14:21–2)
Demon expelled (16:18)	Brethren (16:40)
Publius' father's fever and dysentery (28:8)	All sick on island healed (28:9); church started according to church historians

5. Angelic visitation:
   Example Peter (12:7);
   Paul (27:23–4)

Appendix B

1. Christian DeWet, 'Signs and Wonders in Church Growth' (Masters thesis, School of World Mission, Fuller Theological Seminary, December 1981), 93–123.
2. Ibid., 95–6, 98 (note 3).
3. Ibid., 96–7.
4. Donald O. Young, 'Signs and Wonders and Church

Growth in the Ivory Coast' (Paper written for MC:510, 'Signs, Wonders, and Church Growth', Fuller Theological Seminary, 1982).

5. Donald McGavran, 'Healing and Evangelization of the World' (Syllabus, Basilia Church Growth Seminar, 1979), 296.

6. DeWet, 'Signs and Wonders', 102, 106; cf. 'But What About Hicks?' *Christian Century*, 7 July 1954, 814–15.

7. Donald McGavran, 'Divine Healing and Church Growth', (Address delivered to a gathering of Christian and Missionary Alliance missionaries, Lincoln, Nebraska, 1979).

8. R. R. Cunville, 'The Evangelization of Northeast India' (D. Miss. thesis, School of World Mission, Fuller Seminary, 1975), 156–79.

9. G. Elford, 'Signs and Wonders Among the Canadian Indians' (Paper written for MC:510, 'Signs, Wonders, and Church Growth', Fuller Theological Seminary, 1983).

Appendix C

1. David B. Barrett, 'Global Statistics of the Pentecostal/ Charismatic Renewal', *Ministries Today 1991 Church Resource Directory*, 9.

2. Donald G. Bloesch, *Essentials of Evangelical Theology*, vol. 2, (San Francisco: Harper & Row, 1978), 289.

3. Benjamin B. Warfield, *Counterfeit Miracles* (Edinburgh: The Banner of Truth Trust, 1918).

4. John MacArthur, *The Charismatics* (Grand Rapids, MI: Zondervan, 1978), 131.

5. F. F. Bruce *1 & 2 Corinthians* (London: Marshall, Morgan and Scott, 1971), 122. 'Perfection' here refers to the second coming of Christ. This interpretation appears to fit well within the overall context of 1 Corinthians, especially 1:7: 'Therefore you do not lack any spiritual gift as you eagerly wait for our Lord Jesus Christ to be revealed.' See also Wayne Grudem, *The*

Gift of Prophecy in the New Testament and Today (Eastbourne: Kingsway, 1988), 227–52.
6. James Davison Hunter, *American Evangelicalism* (New Brunswick, NJ: Rutgers University Press, 1980), 41–8.
7. Wagner, 'A Third Wave?', 4–5.

SELECT BIBLIOGRAPHY

Baird, Henry. *The Huguenots*. New York: Charles Scribner, 1895.

Baring-Gould, S. *The Lives of the Saints*. London: John Nimmo, 1897.

Bartleman, Frank. *Azusa Street*. Plainfield: Logos, 1980.

Blamires, Harry. *The Christian Mind*. London: SPCK, 1963.

Bloesch, Donald G. *Essentials of Evangelical Theology*. San Francisco: Harper & Row, 1978.

Brown, Colin, ed. *New International Dictionary of New Testament Theology*. Exeter: Paternoster Press, 1976.

Bruce, F. F. *1 and 2 Corinthians*. London: Marshall, Morgan and Scott, 1971.

The Catholic Encyclopedia Dictionary. New York: The Gilmary Society, 1941.

Coxe, A. Cleveland. *The Ante-Nicene Fathers*. Grand Rapids, MI: Wm B. Eerdmans, 1951.

Cullmann, Oscar. *Christ and Time*. Philadelphia: Westminster Press, 1964.

Defferari, Joseph, ed. *The Fathers of the Church*. Vol. 9, St Basil, *Ancetial Works*. Vol. 15, *Early Christian Biographies*. Vol. 24, St Augustine, *City of God, Books 17–22*. Vol. 25, St Hilary of Poitiers, *The Trinity*. Vol. 39, St Gregory the Great, *Dialogues*. Vol. 44, St Ambrose, *Theological and Dogmatic Works*. Vol. 58, St Gregory of Nyssa, *Ascetical Works*. Washington, DC: The Catholic University of America Press, 1947.

Douglas, J. D., ed. *The New International Dictionary of the Christian Church*. Exeter: Paternoster Press, 1974.

Dudden, F. Homes. *Gregory the Great*. New York: Russell & Russell, 1905.

Dunn, James D. G. *Jesus and the Spirit*. London: SCM Press, 1975.

Engel, James, and Wilbert Norton. *What's Gone Wrong with the Harvest?* Grand Rapids, MI: Zondervan, 1975.

Evangelicals and Social Concern, An Evangelical Commitment. Grand Rapids Report No. 21, 1982.

Fox, George. *The Journal of George Fox*. London: Friends Tract Association, 1901.

Frazier, Claude, ed. *Faith Healing: Finger of God? or Scientific Curiosity?* New York: Thomas Nelson, 1973.

Gordon, A. J. *The Ministry of Healing*. Harrisburg: Christian Publications, Inc., 1802.

Grudem, Wayne. *The Gift of Prophecy in the New Testament and Today*. Eastbourne: Kingsway, 1988.

Hermann, Placid, ed. *St Francis of Assisi*. Chicago: Herald Press, n.d.

Hunter, James Davison. *American Evangelicalism*. New Brunswick, NJ: Rutgers University Press, 1980.

Johnston, Robert K., ed. *The Use of the Bible in Theology – Evangelical Options*. Atlanta, GA: John Knox Press, 1985.

Kallas, James. *The Real Satan*. Minneapolis: Augsburg Publishing House, 1975.

Kittel, G., ed. *Theological Dictionary of the New Testament*. Grand Rapids, MI: Eerdmans, 1964.

Kraft, Charles H. *Christianity and Culture*. Maryknoll, NY: Orbis Books, 1979.

Kraft, Charles H. *Christianity with Power*. Ann Arbor, MI: Vine, 1989.

Kreiser, Robert. *Miracles, Convulsions, and Ecclesiastical Politics in Early Eighteenth-Century Paris*. Princeton: Princeton University Press, 1978.

Ladd, George Eldon. *The Presence of the Future*. Grand Rapids, MI: Eerdmans, 1974.

Ladd, George Eldon. *A Theology of the New Testament*. Guildford: Lutterworth Press, 1974.

Langton, Edward. *Essentials of Demonology: A Study of Jewish and Christian Doctrine, Its Origin and Development*. London: Epworth Press, 1949.

Laurentin, Rene. *Miracles in El Paso*. Ann Arbor, MI: Servant, 1982.

Lloyd-Jones, D. Martyn. *Joy Unspeakable*. Eastbourne: Kingsway, 1984.

MacArthur, John. *The Charismatics*. Grand Rapids, MI: Zondervan, 1978.

Newbigin, Lesslie. *Foolishness to the Greeks: The Gospel and Western Culture*. London: SPCK, 1986.

Oswald, Hilton, ed. *Luther's Works*. Saint Louis: Concordia Publishing House, n.d.

Rahner, Karl. *Spiritual Exercises*. London: Herder & Herder, 1962.

Ridderbos, Herman. *The Coming of the Kingdom*. Philadelphia: Presbyterian and Reformed, 1962.

Schnackenburg, Rudolf. *The Moral Teaching of the New Testament*. New York: Seabury, 1965.

Sire, James. *The Universe Next Door*. Leicester: IVP, 1977.

Sogaard, Viggo. *Everything You Need to Know for a Cassette Ministry*. Minneapolis, MN: Bethany Publishing Company, 1975.

Tappert, Theodore B., ed. *Luther: Letters of Spiritual Counsel*. The Library of Christian Classics, vol. 18. Philadelphia: Westminster Press, n.d.

Telford, John, ed. *The Letters of John Wesley*. London: Epworth Press, 1931.

Tippett, Alan R. *People Movements in Southern Polynesia*. Chicago: Moody Press, 1971.

Wagner, C. Peter. *Church Growth and the Whole Gospel*. New York: Harper & Row, 1981.

Warfield, Benjamin B. *Counterfeit Miracles*. Edinburgh: The Banner of Truth Trust, 1918.

Wesley, John. *The Works of John Wesley*, 3rd ed. Peabody, MA: Hendrickson Publishers, 1984.

Wilkinson, John. *Health and Healing*. New York: Columbia University Press, 1980.

Wimber, John, and Kevin Springer. *Power Healing*. London: Hodder & Stoughton, 1986.